D1761565

PLAIN
&
Fancy

A Cookbook by
the Junior League
of Richardson, Texas

JUNIOR LEAGUE
R I C H A R D S O N

The Junior League of Richardson promotes volunteerism through the
training and education of its members. Its logo is a heart framed by leaves,
with the heart symbolizing the services provided by League volunteers and
the leaves representing the personal growth that comes from the volunteer
experience.

Copyright 1984
Junior League of Richardson, Incorporated
Richardson, Texas
All Rights Reserved

First Printing   July 1984   15,000 copies
Library of Congress Catalog Card Number 83-082689
I S B N   0-9612810-0-6

Additional copies may be obtained by addressing:

PLAIN AND FANCY
Junior League of Richardson, Inc.
P.O. Box 835808
Richardson, Texas   75083

Printed by Hart Graphics, Inc.
Austin, Texas

Richardson, Texas is part of the fastest growing area in metropolitan Dallas. In true melting pot fashion, new residents come not only from neighboring cities but also from all over the United States and abroad. The result is a suburban community with a highly diversified outlook.

Plain and Fancy reflects that diversity. On the one hand, it offers shortcuts to quality. On the other, it highlights the creative side of cooking. The following pages are filled with hundreds of easy, make ahead dishes, satisfying "quick fix" meals and innovative recipes that let you show off your culinary skills . . . all of them a reflection of the way we cook today.

Like other communities, the Richardson lifestyle is fast and friendly and fun. For everyone who, at one time or another, doubles as nurse and nanny, homemaker and helpmate, chef and chauffeur, corporate v.p. and community volunteer, we dedicate this book to you.

Special thanks to:
Buford Barr, McCann-Erickson, Inc.
Dorian Wall, Design Art Director
Don Heit, Photographer
Jean Compton Dennis, Copywriter
Nan Mulvaney, Hart Graphics, Inc.
Teresa Cage, Editor
Cosette McGee, Food Stylist
Ivy House, Old Town

COOKBOOK CO-CHAIRMEN:
Audrey Godfrey Beasley
Cissy Holloway Burnam
Kitty Howard Hamby

COOKBOOK COMMITTEE MEMBERS:
Debby Dixon Amis
Cary Conner Burchak
Joanne Clay Cure
Missy Ingham Edwards
Anne Gibson Forsey
Charlotte Lawson Frazier
Katy Coplin Glidewell
Linda Brooke Grona
Susan Rentfro Gummer
Josephine Therrell "Pokey" Gustafson
Terri Tiffany Hamric
Sharon Clifton Jones
Lori Root Kircher
Kathy Harlan Klickman
Lynette Mann Landry
Jean Klingaman Lawson
Julie Andrews McAllister
Linda Sample McCarley
Jan Holloway Miller
Mindy Courtin Myers
Jo Davidson Paxton
Melody Miller Rice
Barbara Strait Smyth
Elizabeth Jane Stephens
Becky Stubblefield Wagner
Anne Quekemeyer Wall
Sue Penn Ward

COOKBOOK COMMITTEE CHAIRMEN:
Cheryl Pracht Bond — Office
Pam McClain Clarke — Wholesale
Lynn Schwarzer Cooper — Retail
Lucy Newton Doty — Assistant Office
Marsha Spencer Gearing — Proofreading
Barbara Collier Sponberg — Retail
Janice Giddens Staples — Retail
Janet Rumbaugh Young — Promotion

LIAISONS:
Cheri Wood Clark
Pat Hall Collins
Charlotte McCarty Fowler
Pat Mullin Knott
Maureen Murphy Lewis
Vicki Albritton Midyett
Melissa Stallcup Vauthier

ACKNOWLEDGEMENTS

CONTRIBUTORS:

Jan Tonelli Ahders
Carol Crane Allen
Susan Elkins Allen
Peggy Olson Anderson
Linda Gaston Andre
Char Anderson Ankeney
Mary Nelle Vincent
  Armstrong
Patty Jones Atchley
Betty Dorsey Baird
Marty Hauschild Baker
Maryted Lokey Banta
Gayle Pierson Barnes
Lyle Spencer Barr
Carol White Barry
Ann Ockerman Baughn
Donna Evans Beaver
Sandra Cupp Bell
Susan Ezell Bell
Glenda LaBrot Blankenship
Alice Maze Bogden
Diane Erickson Bown
Jennifer Locke Braasch
Terry Bolding Brown
Laura English Burnett
Celia Tapp Burros
Nancy Phillips Burton
Carla Peters Byrom
Donna Rohning Carruth
Barbie Brown Casey
Lana Shehee Cass
Dorothy Marsh Cheairs
Judith Von Gautschi Clarke
Barbie Morgan Coleman
Gail Shaddock Cook
Susan Jones Copeland
Liz Davis Cross
Donna Dale
Betsy Holt Davis
Linda Boon Defee
Gayle Thompson Denton
Mary Bruce Featherston
  DeVoe
Dolly Mercadal Deibel
Eileen Flaherty Diggin
Lynne Boylan Dildy
Beverly Robbins Dobat
Teresa Montgomery Dodson
Judy Stewart Ducate
Jane Wiginton Edwards
Marsha Klein Emmett
Linda Jo Davis Evans
Billie Bish Fargo
Margery Erhardt Feller
Pam Lorette Field
Suzanne Bachand Fitzgerald
Candy Stringer Fraley
Julie Roberts Francis
Suzanne Sims Frederiksen

Linda Foster Gadd
Nancy Benko Gamble
Judy Croak Garlick
Lynda Miller Garrett
Eunice Greenblatt Gerard
Patty Fisher Giles
Patricia Vote Gill
Pam Smith Graves
Annette Teer Griffin
Mary Lewis Grubbs
Christi McCarroll Guion
Louise Mugford Hager
Phyllis Haley
Rowanne Leckenby Haley
Helen Plopa Hardwick
Betty Snipes Harper
Dorin Edgar Harrison
Judy Stevenson Hassack
Grace Brown Hatch
Margaret Coco Hawthorne
Kathy Satterthwaite Heick
Molly Ziegelmeyer Helling
Cynthia Wendland
  Henderson
Judi Buschbaum Hensley
Harriet Asman Hetzler
Pam Thompson Holmes
Kathleen Louapre Howell
Ann Bonham Hubbard
Virginia Warfield Humphries
Elizabeth Connelly Jackson
Elizabeth Hopkins Jackson
Linda Beck Jackson
Ollie Schmidt Johnson
Silkie Warthan Justice
Pat Barber Kepner
Gene Ann Parker Kirby
Lana Lewallen Kiser
Donna Conaster Koller
Carol Gantt Koschak
Pam Andberg Krause
Terry Ballinger Landry
Nancy Pearson Lang
Glenda Hairston Ledford
Barbara Smith Leopard
Carolyn Pavletich Lesh
Carole Cornwell Lieving
Jane Bradley Livingston
Kandy Hensley Logan
Jody Konesky Maslen
Sally Prados McAfee
Sandra Marshall McAteer
Peggy Burns McBurnett
Linda Webster McCall
Meredy Mason McClure
Susan Wehmeyer McCrory
Brenda Tucker McDonald
Beth Sours McIntire
Dorthy Holmes McKearin

Judith Lamontagne McPhail
Jennifer Jeffreys McVay
Jennifer Whitten Metzger
Juli Higgins Middlekauff
Renee Spencer Miller
Lynda Brown Moegling
Susan Horner Molina
Maxine Watson Moody
Liz Bowell Moore
Jenny Moore
Sharon Williams Newbold
Marilyn Storm Nichols
Ruth Nix Norton
Karen Wijas Pennington
Sarah Jean Howard Pfeiffer
Judi Lawrence Pierson
Mary Ann Ketron Pittman
Audrey Warren Plummer
Tanda Brumfield Pohl
Jo Weigel Ragan
Edanna Watson Reagor
Leslie Turner Rippamonti
Sun Ann Long Roberts
Penny Jerrell Romig
Mary Barter Roop
Donna Luke Sands
Garice Peek Schneider
Annette Lasser Schnieders
Phyllis Dunlap Shaddock
Diann Tessman Slaton
Arleen Durkee Smith
Pat Ehrich Smothermon
Claudia Mendenhall Sommer
Dolores Mullenix Spence
Kathleen Spence Stallings
Linda Beyers Steelman
Kathy Easton Stewart
Pamela Lucas Stokes
Jan Post Stubblefield
Charlotte Becker Sullivan
Courtney Tyler Tanner
Emily Russell Tarr
Mary Gail Hall Thomas
Linda Kleber Tubbs
Betsey Carr Tweddale
Sandra Solly Utz
Paula Sandrude Van Vleck
Kay Brown White
Janice West Whitehill
Gail Lane Williams
Sally Smith Williams
Faye Ratherber Willis
Sharon Schnase Wilson
Judith Austin Wimpey
Sue Harvey Woods
LeAnne Duckworth
  Worsham
Linda Neff Ziegler

PLAIN
MENUS

"The Buffet Bowl"
New Year's Day

Holiday Eggnog
Party Scramble
Chili Biscuits
New Year's Eve Dip
Smoked Turkey Ball
Curry Dip with Raw Vegetables
Easy Pecan Loaf

"On the Patio, at the Park"
4th of July Cookout

Southern Mint Juleps
Fourth of July Potato Salad
Grilled Vegetable Packets
Lemonade Chicken
Crusty French Bread with Herb Butter
Country Vanilla Ice Cream

MENUS

" 'Tis Better to Give"
Christmas Treats

White Chocolate Cranberries
Sherried Walnuts
Merry Meringue Christmas Cookies
Christmas Morning Cinnamon Rolls
Blackberry Wine Cake

"Light and Luscious"
League Luncheon

Tea Sippers
Ham and Asparagus Rolls
Pretzel Fruit Salad
Stuffed Mushrooms with Spinach
Blueberry Tea Muffins
Mocha Mousse Cake

PLAIN
MENUS

"If I'd Known You Were Comin' . . ."
A Meal from the Freezer

New Potato Skins
Paper Cup Frozen Salad
Beef Tortini
No Fail Refrigerator Rolls
Pralines 'n Cream Pie

"The Morning Glory Group"
A Neighborhood Coffee

Tea Sandwiches
Butterscotch Pecan Rolls
Frosted Egg Mold
Easy Cinnamon Crisps
Coffee

MENUS

"The Pleasure of Your Company"
Dinner at Eight

Shrimp Filled Artichokes
Fresh Fruit in Season with French Salad Dressing
Very Special Fresh Vegetables
Poulet Dijonnaise in Phyllo
Dinner Rolls
Amaretto Cheesecake

"Putting Your Best Feast Forward"
Holiday Family Gathering

Wild Rice Soup
Cranberry Eggnog Layered Salad
Herbed Roast Leg of Lamb
Glazed Carrots and Grapes
Baked Natural Asparagus
Dinner Rolls
Steamed Christmas Pudding with Lemon Sauce

PLAIN
MENUS

"Home on the Range"
A Southwestern Supper

Margaritas by the Gallon
Mexican Cheese Ball
Brisket in a Bag with Barbecue Sauce
Jalapeno Baked Potatoes
Congealed Avocado Salad
Mexican Chocolate Cake with Praline Frosting

"For Teens 'n Tweens"
Pizza Pizzazz

Pizza Dip
Towering Pizza
Spaghetti Salad
Italian Carrots
Cherry Pizza

MENUS

"A Chilling Experience"
Summertime Buffet

Vineyard Punch
Stuffed Snow Peas
Chilled Cantaloupe Soup
Lemon Ring Green Beans
Party Rolls
English Trifle

"The All Occasion Celebration"
Sunday Brunch

Orange Blossoms
Crab Stuffed Pastry
Stuffed Eggs au Gratin
Caramel Sticky Rolls
Hot Sherried Fruit

How to put holidays on ice

Beef Stroganoff Dip

New idea from a seasoned entree

1 ½ pounds ground chuck
1 large onion, chopped
Seasoned salt to taste
Garlic salt to taste
Pepper to taste
8 ounces cream cheese, softened
8 ounces tomato sauce
¼ cup catsup
5 tablespoons picante sauce
1 tablespoon oregano
Corn chips

In large frying pan, brown chuck with onion, seasoned salt, garlic salt and pepper. Pour off grease. Add cream cheese, tomato sauce, catsup, picante sauce and oregano, mixing well. Heat slowly and stir until mixture is well blended. Serve in chafing dish with chips. *May be prepared ahead.*

Serves 8

Fiesta Dip

Armchair quarterback winner

1 pound ground chuck
2 large yellow onions, chopped
15 ounces canned kidney beans
3 tablespoons chili powder
14 ounces hot catsup
2 red onions, chopped
⅓ cup chopped ripe olives
½ cup pitted green olives, chopped
2 cups grated sharp Cheddar cheese
Tortilla chips

In large frying pan, brown chuck with yellow onions. Drain and set aside. Mash kidney beans and mix with chili powder and catsup. Combine meat and bean mixtures and transfer to chafing dish liner. Mix red onions, ripe olives and green olives and spread over meat mixture. Top with cheese and bake at 325° until cheese is melted. Serve in chafing dish with chips. *May be prepared ahead.*

Serves 12

Beef Picadillo
South of the border dip

1 pound ground beef
1 pound ground pork
2 teaspoons salt
½ teaspoon pepper
14 ounces diced pimiento
1½ cups chopped almonds
1½ cups golden raisins
5 garlic cloves, minced
1 bunch green onions, chopped
4 jalapeno peppers, seeded and chopped
½ teaspoon oregano
2 tablespoons cumin
16 ounces stewed tomatoes
12 ounces tomato paste
Tortilla chips

In large frying pan or stock pot, brown beef and pork and pour off grease. Add salt, pepper and just enough water to cover. Simmer for 30 minutes. Add the following ingredients 1 at a time, stirring after each addition: pimiento, almonds, raisins, garlic, green onions, jalapeno peppers, oregano, cumin, stewed tomatoes and tomato paste. Cover and simmer for 45 minutes or until slightly thickened. Serve in chafing dish with chips. *May be prepared ahead. May be frozen.*

Serves 12

Anchovy Dip
For those distinguished palates

1 cup mayonnaise
8 ounces cream cheese, softened
3 tablespoons anchovy paste
⅓ cup snipped parsley
3 tablespoons chopped chives
1 garlic clove, pressed
1 tablespoon lemon juice
2 tablespoons tarragon vinegar
Salt to taste
Pepper to taste
Raw vegetables

With mixer, blend mayonnaise and cream cheese. Add anchovy paste, parsley, chives, garlic, lemon juice, vinegar, salt and pepper, stirring well. Serve with vegetables. *May be prepared ahead.*

Serves 12

Gourmet Shrimp Dip

Favorite party fare

1 cup small curd cottage cheese
½ cup mayonnaise
4 ounces canned shrimp, drained
1 small onion, minced
⅛ teaspoon garlic salt
½ teaspoon Worcestershire sauce
¾ teaspoon prepared mustard
½ teaspoon celery seed
Crackers or chips

Blend all ingredients except crackers or chips. Cover and refrigerate for at least 5 hours. Serve with crackers or chips. *Must be prepared ahead.*

Serves 8

Dilly Shrimp Dip

Tempting flavor

24 ounces cream cheese, softened
2 tablespoons lemon juice
2 tablespoons dill
½ cup mayonnaise
½ cup butter, softened
1 teaspoon seasoned salt
Cayenne pepper to taste
1 onion, chopped
16 ounces canned shrimp, drained
Crackers

With mixer, blend cream cheese, lemon juice, dill, mayonnaise, butter, seasoned salt and cayenne pepper. Stir in onion and shrimp. Serve with crackers. *May be prepared ahead.*

Serves 20

Crab Ring Delight
Rich and ritzy

¼ cup water
1 teaspoon unflavored gelatin
16 ounces cream cheese, softened
2 tablespoons cooking sherry
¾ teaspoon seasoned salt
2 ounces diced pimiento, drained
6 ounces fresh or frozen crabmeat
⅛ teaspoon pepper
2 tablespoons snipped parsley
Parsley sprigs
Crackers

Heat water in double boiler. Sprinkle gelatin over water and stir until dissolved. Blend gelatin and cream cheese. Stir in sherry, seasoned salt, pimiento, crabmeat, pepper and snipped parsley. Pour into greased 3 cup ring mold and refrigerate for 4 hours or until set. Garnish with parsley sprigs. Serve with crackers. *Must be prepared ahead.*

Serves 16

Egg Salad Party Dip
Something new for veggies

½ cup mayonnaise
8 ounces cream cheese, softened
1 egg, hard boiled and finely chopped
2 tablespoons chopped onion
Pepper to taste
⅛ teaspoon garlic powder
Snipped parsley to taste
Raw vegetables

With mixer, blend mayonnaise and cream cheese. Add egg, onion, pepper, garlic powder and parsley, mixing well. Serve with vegetables. *May be prepared ahead.*

Serves 12

New Year's Eve Dip
A Texas tradition

1 onion, chopped
4 tablespoons butter
4 cups grated Monterey Jack cheese
30 ounces canned black eyed peas with jalapeno peppers
Tortilla chips

In large frying pan or saucepan, saute onion in butter until soft. Add cheese and black eyed peas, stirring until cheese is melted and mixture is thoroughly heated. Serve in chafing dish with chips. *May be prepared ahead.*

Serves 10

Black Eyed Pea Dip
Southern dippin' at its best

¼ cup finely chopped green pepper
8 jalapeno peppers, finely chopped
2 celery ribs, finely chopped
1 large onion, minced
2 tablespoons Tabasco sauce
½ cup catsup
1 teaspoon salt
1 teaspoon coarsely ground pepper
3 chicken bouillon cubes
¼ teaspoon nutmeg
¼ teaspoon cinnamon
30 ounces canned black eyed peas
14 ounces canned whole tomatoes, chopped
1 teaspoon garlic powder
½ cup bacon drippings
3 tablespoons flour
Tortilla chips

In large saucepan, mix green pepper, jalapeno peppers, celery, onion, Tabasco sauce, catsup, salt, pepper, bouillon cubes, nutmeg and cinnamon. Bring to a slow simmer over low heat. Add black eyed peas, tomatoes and garlic and continue cooking for 30 minutes. In small bowl, blend bacon drippings with flour. Stir into peas and simmer for 10 minutes. Serve in chafing dish with chips. *May be prepared ahead.*

Serves 16

Savory Spinach Dip
Plays a dual role. . .also an omelet filling

10 ounces frozen chopped spinach, thawed and drained
½ cup parsley flakes
1 bunch green onions, chopped
½ tablespoon dill
½ tablespoon seasoned salt
1 cup mayonnaise
1 cup sour cream
4 ounces cream cheese, softened
2 tablespoons lemon juice
Oregano to taste
Pepper to taste
Basil to taste
Raw vegetables

Blend all ingredients except raw vegetables. Cover and refrigerate for at least 6 hours. Serve as dip with vegetables. *Must be prepared ahead.*

Serves 12

White Guacamole
Everyone wll rush to this one

¾ cup mayonnaise
¾ cup sour cream
3 tablespoons canned chopped green chilies, drained
1 tomato, finely chopped and drained
2 tablespoons lemon juice
2 avocados, mashed
Garlic salt to taste
Salt to taste
Pepper to taste
Tortilla chips

Blend all ingredients except tortilla chips. Cover and refrigerate for at least 1 hour. Serve with chips. *Must be prepared ahead.*

Serves 12

Guacamole

Si, si, Senor

3 to 4 avocados, mashed
1 tablespoon picante sauce
½ teaspoon garlic powder
1 tablespoon lemon juice
1 onion, chopped
1 tomato, chopped
Salt to taste
Pepper to taste
Tortilla chips

Blend all ingredients except tortilla chips. Serve with chips.

Serves 8

Pizza Dip

Wow

8 ounces cream cheese, softened
1 cup chili sauce
1 green pepper, chopped
3 tablespoons chopped red onion
½ pound fresh mushrooms, chopped
2 cups grated mozzarella cheese
Sourdough bread rounds

Cover bottom of shallow serving dish with cream cheese. Top with chili sauce. Separately layer green pepper, red onion, mushrooms and mozzarella cheese. Serve with thinly sliced bread rounds. *May be prepared ahead.*

Serves 12

Curry Dip
For curry haters

¾ cup mayonnaise
4½ tablespoons minced onion
4½ tablespoons catsup
4½ tablespoons honey
1½ tablespoons lemon juice
1½ tablespoons curry powder
Raw vegetables

Blend all ingredients except raw vegetables. Cover and refrigerate for 2 days. Serve with vegetables. *Must be prepared ahead.*

Serves 8

Chicken Cracklings
Finger lickin' good

4 pounds boneless chicken breast, cubed
1 cup soy sauce
½ cup lemon juice
1 teaspoon salt
1½ cups oil for frying
3 cups flour
½ tablespoon paprika
1 teaspoon coarsely ground pepper

Marinate chicken in mixture of soy sauce, lemon juice and salt for 6 to 8 hours, turning frequently. Heat oil in large frying pan. Mix flour, paprika and pepper. Drain chicken, coat well with flour mixture and cook in hot oil until crisp and brown. Drain and serve in chafing dish. *Must be prepared ahead. May be frozen and reheated by placing frozen chicken on baking sheet. Cover with foil and puncture for release of steam. Bake until chicken is thoroughly heated.*

Serves 8

Shrimp Nibbles
Canapes men will remember

1 cup mayonnaise
1 cup grated Cheddar cheese
Triscuits
4 ounces canned shrimp, drained

Blend mayonnaise with cheese and set aside. Arrange Triscuits on baking sheet. Top with 1 or 2 shrimp and 1 teaspoon cheese mixture. Broil until cheese is melted. *Filling may be prepared ahead.*

Serves 8

Party Seafood Quiche

Real men will eat this quiche

Pastry for 2 crust pie
6 ounces fresh or frozen crabmeat or shrimp
1 cup grated Swiss cheese
1 cup grated Monterey Jack cheese
1 onion, thinly sliced
2 tablespoons butter
6 eggs, lightly beaten
3 cups whipping cream
½ cup dry sherry
1 tablespoon salt
1 teaspoon nutmeg
½ teaspoon white pepper

Line 15x10 inch jelly roll pan with pastry. Cover with waxed paper and sprinkle with dried beans or rice to hold crust in place while baking. Bake at 425° for 5 minutes. Discard beans or rice and waxed paper. Set crust aside to cool. Mix crabmeat with Swiss cheese and Monterey Jack cheese and set aside. Saute onion in butter and set aside. In large bowl, blend eggs, whipping cream, sherry, salt, nutmeg and white pepper. Add onion and mix well. Spread crabmeat mixture on crust and top with egg and cream mixture. Bake at 425° for 15 minutes. Reduce heat to 325° and bake for 20 minutes or until done. Cut into 1x2 inch rectangles for appetizers or 8 dinner size servings. *May be prepared ahead.*

Serves 20

Crab Stuffed Pastry

Easy come, easy go

½ cup butter, softened
3 ounces cream cheese, softened
1 cup flour
6 ounces canned crabmeat, drained
½ cup grated sharp Cheddar cheese
2 green onions, minced
Seasoned salt to taste
Tabasco sauce to taste
Lemon juice to taste

With mixer, blend butter with cream cheese. Gradually mix in flour then refrigerate dough for 30 minutes. For stuffing, mix crabmeat, cheese, onions, seasoned salt, Tabasco sauce and lemon juice. Set aside. Roll dough into 24 small balls and press into greased miniature muffin tin cups. Fill with stuffing and bake at 350° for 30 minutes. *May be prepared ahead and refrigerated before filling cups.*

Serves 8

Won Tons

Chinese staple Americans love

½ pound ground pork
¼ cup chopped water chestnuts
1 celery rib, chopped
1 teaspoon ginger juice
1 teaspoon salt
2 teaspoons soy sauce
4 green onions, minced
Pepper to taste
1 pound won ton wrappers
Oil for frying

Mix pork, water chestnuts, celery, ginger juice, salt, soy sauce, onions and pepper. Place 1 teaspoon of filling in center of won ton wrapper. Fold envelope style. To seal edges, moisten with water. Deep fry in hot oil until brown. *May be prepared ahead and may be frozen, reheating in oven.*

Serves 10

Sausage Bites

Pretty miniatures

½ pound hot sausage
2 eggs, lightly beaten
1 cup cottage cheese
1 tablespoon chopped chives
Pepper to taste
¼ cup grated Parmesan cheese
6 canned butterflake dinner rolls

Brown sausage until crumbly, drain and set aside. Mix eggs with cottage cheese, chives, pepper and Parmesan cheese. Set aside. Divide each roll into 8 sections. Thinly roll each section and press into greased miniature muffin tin cups. Add sausage and top with egg mixture. Bake at 350° for 20 minutes or until filling is lightly brown.

Serves 12

Chili Biscuits

Good for lunch, too

40 party size rolls
19 ounces canned chili, heated
5 green onions, chopped
2 cups grated sharp Cheddar cheese

Scoop centers from rolls. Fill with chili, sprinkle with onions and top with cheese. Bake at 375° until cheese is melted. May be served for lunch using larger rolls.

Serves 10

Broccoli Tidbits

A recipe you'll want to share

20 ounces frozen chopped broccoli, thawed and drained

8 ounces herb seasoned stuffing mix

1 large onion, minced

6 eggs, well beaten

¾ cup butter, melted

½ cup freshly grated Parmesan cheese

1 teaspoon pepper

½ tablespoon garlic salt

½ teaspoon thyme

Mix all ingredients and shape into bite size balls. Place on greased baking sheets and heat at 325° for 15 minutes or until brown. *May be prepared ahead. May be frozen before cooking.*

Serves 20

Forget Me Nots

Freezer pleaser

1 pound ground beef

1 pound ground pork

16 ounces Velveeta cheese, diced

1 teaspoon oregano

2 tablespoons Worcestershire sauce

½ teaspoon garlic salt

½ teaspoon Italian seasoning

1 pound party rye bread slices

In frying pan, brown beef and pork. Add cheese, oregano, Worcestershire sauce, garlic salt and Italian seasoning. Cook over low heat, stirring frequently, until cheese is melted. Spread on bread and bake at 350° for 10 minutes or until bubbly. *May be prepared ahead and frozen before baking.*

Serves 16

Esfeha

For the adventurous palate

1 pound ground lamb or beef, well browned and drained
½ cup plain yogurt
½ cup grated Parmesan cheese
Garlic powder to taste
Onion powder to taste
Allspice to taste
Salt to taste
Pepper to taste
20 canned non buttermilk biscuits

In bowl, blend meat, yogurt, Parmesan cheese, garlic powder, onion powder, allspice, salt and pepper. Set aside to cool. On greased baking sheet, flatten each biscuit, leaving lip. Spread with meat mixture and bake at 375° until biscuits brown. *May be prepared ahead and baked just before serving.*

Serves 10

Dove Breasts

Gourmet game

10 dove breasts
10 jalapeno peppers, halved lengthwise and seeded
8 ounces sliced water chestnuts
10 bacon slices, cut in half
Worcestershire sauce to taste
Barbecue sauce (optional)

Place dove breasts in boiling water. Cover, lower heat and cook for 5 minutes. Drain and carefully bone, dividing each breast in ½. Layer jalapeno pepper slice and water chestnut slice on each breast ½. Wrap with bacon and skewer with toothpick. Sprinkle with Worcestershire sauce. Cook in broiler, smoker or on barbecue coals until bacon is done. May be served with barbecue sauce as a dip. *May be prepared ahead and refrigerated before cooking.*

Serves 6

Pineapple Rumaki

Surprise. . .no chicken livers

16 ounces water chestnuts, drained
15 ounces canned pineapple chunks, drained
1 pound sliced bacon, cut in half
1 cup catsup
1 tablespoon teriyaki sauce
1 cup sugar

Wrap water chestnut and pineapple chunk in bacon and skewer with toothpick. Heat in 8 inch square baking dish at 300° for 1 hour. Mix catsup, teriyaki sauce and sugar. Pour over rumaki and heat for 1 hour. *May be prepared ahead.*

Serves 8

Cocktail Franks

Man pleasing hors d'oeuvre

1 cup sour cream
⅓ cup prepared mustard
1 pound cocktail frankfurters

Blend sour cream and mustard. Stir in frankfurters. Bake in 1 quart baking dish at 325° for 30 minutes. Serve in chafing dish. *May be prepared ahead.*

Serves 10

Drunken Wieners

Savory way to serve franks

1 cup bourbon
1 cup confectioners' sugar, sifted
2 cups catsup
Garlic salt to taste
1 tablespoon Worcestershire sauce
2 pounds cocktail frankfurters

In large saucepan, mix bourbon, sugar, catsup, garlic salt and Worcestershire sauce. Add frankfurters and simmer for 40 minutes. Serve in chafing dish. *May be prepared ahead.*

Serves 20

Smoked Turkey Ball

What a way to use leftovers

1 ½ cups finely ground smoked turkey
8 ounces cream cheese, softened
3 tablespoons mayonnaise
½ cup chopped pecans
2 tablespoons snipped parsley
Triscuits

With mixer, blend turkey, cream cheese and mayonnaise. Chill. Shape into ball and roll in pecans and parsley. Serve with Triscuits. *Must be prepared ahead.*

Serves 12

Danish Meatballs

Serve sandwich style with party rolls

¾ pound ground beef
¼ pound ground pork
1 small onion, grated
½ cup dry bread crumbs
1 teaspoon salt
¼ teaspoon pepper
⅛ teaspoon nutmeg
⅛ teaspoon marjoram
2 eggs
½ cup milk
3 tablespoons shortening
10 ounces beef consomme
Party size rolls (optional)

Lightly mix beef, pork, onion, bread crumbs, salt, pepper, nutmeg, marjoram, eggs and milk. Shape into 4 dozen balls. In large frying pan, heat shortening and brown meatballs. Pour off grease. Add consomme, cover and simmer for 15 minutes. Reserving liquid in frying pan, remove meatballs to chafing dish and cover with sauce. *May be prepared ahead. Meatballs may be frozen.*

Serves 8

Sauce

2 tablespoons flour
3 tablespoons water
2 tablespoons sweet relish

Add water to reserved liquid in frying pan for 1 cupful. Heat to boiling. Blend flour with 3 tablespoons water and stir into frying pan. Cook, stirring continuously, to boiling. Continue boiling for 1 minute. Stir in relish.

Curried Meatballs

Indian flavor Americanized

1 ½ pounds ground beef
1 ½ pounds ground pork
3 eggs
1 ½ cups dry bread crumbs
1 large onion, chopped
Garlic salt to taste
Pepper to taste
Oregano to taste
Thyme to taste
Cayenne pepper to taste
Snipped parsley to taste
Oil for frying

Mix beef, pork, eggs, bread crumbs, onion, garlic salt, pepper, oregano, thyme, cayenne pepper and parsley. Shape into small balls and brown in hot oil. Drain. Pour sauce over meatballs and serve in chafing dish. *May be prepared ahead. Meatballs may be frozen.*

Serves 20

Sauce

1 bunch green onions, chopped
1 cup butter
1 tablespoon curry
½ tablespoon ginger
½ garlic clove, minced
Salt to taste
Pepper to taste
Tabasco sauce to taste
20 ounces cream of chicken soup
10 ounces cream of mushroom soup
10 ounces cream of celery soup
¼ cup sherry
¼ cup milk (optional)

In large saucepan, saute onions in butter with curry, ginger, garlic, salt, pepper and Tabasco sauce. Stir in soups and heat thoroughly. Stir in sherry. For thinner sauce, stir in milk.

31

Saucy Meatballs
Anything goes

3 pounds ground round or chuck
1 teaspoon salt
½ teaspoon pepper
1 cup dry bread crumbs
2 eggs
1 onion, chopped
2 bacon slices
24 ounces chili sauce
13 ounces cranberry sauce

Mix meat, salt, pepper, bread crumbs, eggs and onion. Shape into small balls. In frying pan, cook bacon. Drain, reserving drippings in pan, and crumble. Brown meatballs in drippings. Pour off grease. Mix chili sauce, cranberry sauce and bacon. Add to meatballs. Cover and simmer for 1 hour. *Meatballs may be prepared ahead and may be frozen.*

Serves 12

Ceviche
Seafood at its freshest

½ pound scallops, cubed
½ pound white fish, cubed
1 cup lemon juice
2 large onions, chopped
1 cup tomato juice
1 teaspoon salt
½ teaspoon pepper
½ teaspoon oregano
½ teaspoon Tabasco sauce
2 tablespoons snipped parsley
¾ cup catsup
2 tablespoons Worcestershire sauce
¼ pound shrimp, cooked and peeled
Crackers

Marinate scallops and white fish in lemon juice for 2 hours. Drain, reserving lemon juice. In large bowl, mix onions, tomato juice, salt, pepper, oregano, Tabasco sauce, parsley, catsup and Worcestershire sauce. Fold in scallops and white fish. Adjust taste with reserved lemon juice. Cover and refrigerate overnight. Add shrimp 2 hours before serving. Serve cold with crackers. *Must be prepared ahead.*

Serves 6

Stuffed Mushrooms with Spinach

Boursin cheese makes the difference

24 large fresh mushroom caps

2 tablespoons oil

10 ounces frozen chopped spinach, cooked and drained

10 ounces Boursin cheese, softened

Seasoned bread crumbs

Brush mushroom caps with oil. Place on baking sheet, round side up, and broil for 1 minute. Blend spinach with cheese and fill mushroom caps. Sprinkle with bread crumbs and bake on greased baking sheet at 375° for 10 minutes or until bubbly. Serve immediately. *May be frozen and baked unthawed.*

Serves 8

Shrimp Filled Mushrooms

Neptune's delight

24 large fresh mushrooms

1 onion, chopped

¼ cup butter

½ pound shrimp, cooked, peeled and chopped

4 ounces blue cheese

½ teaspoon basil

Remove stems from mushrooms, reserving ½. Chop reserved stems and saute with onion in butter. Add shrimp, blue cheese and basil, mixing well. Stuff mushroom caps with shrimp mixture and broil for 5 minutes or until cheese bubbles.

Serves 8

Bacon Stuffed Mushrooms

Don't pass this up

10 bacon slices
¾ cup mayonnaise
1 onion, chopped
1½ cups grated sharp Cheddar cheese
Seasoned salt to taste
3 pints fresh mushrooms, stems removed

Fry bacon, drain and crumble. Blend with mayonnaise, onion, cheese and seasoned salt. Fill mushroom caps with cheese mixture and place on greased baking sheet. Cover and bake at 325° for 15 minutes or until cheese bubbles. *May be prepared ahead.*

Serves 16

Mushroom Croustades

Easy gourmet treat

24 thin white bread slices
2 tablespoons butter, melted
2 tablespoons minced onion
1 small garlic clove, minced
4 tablespoons butter
½ pound fresh mushrooms, finely chopped
3 tablespoons flour
1 cup whipping cream
½ teaspoon salt
⅛ teaspoon cayenne pepper
1 tablespoon snipped parsley
1½ tablespoons chopped chives
½ tablespoon lemon juice
2 tablespoons grated Parmesan cheese

Cut 3 inch round from each bread slice. Using 2 tablespoons butter, coat muffin tin cups. Carefully mold bread into cups and bake at 350° until lightly brown. Set aside to cool. To prepare filling, saute onion and garlic in 4 tablespoons butter until soft but not brown. Stir in mushrooms and cook for 10 minutes or until all moisture has evaporated. Remove from heat, sprinkle with flour and blend well. Add whipping cream and return to heat. Cook, stirring continuously, until mixture comes to a boil. Reduce heat and simmer for 2 minutes. Remove from heat and mix with salt, cayenne pepper, parsley, chives and lemon juice. Fill cups with mushroom mixture, top with Parmesan cheese and bake at 350° for 10 minutes. Broil to brown tops. *May be prepared 2 hours ahead and refrigerated before baking. Filling and shells may be frozen separately.*

Serves 8

Parmesan Onion Rounds

Here one minute. . .gone the next

1 cup mayonnaise
3 tablespoons grated Parmesan cheese
24 party rye or white bread rounds
1 small onion, separated into rings

Blend mayonnaise with Parmesan cheese. Spread on bread rounds and top with onion rings. Broil until brown and bubbly. *Filling may be prepared ahead.*

Serves 8

Caponata

Eggplant relish from the Mediterranean

¾ pound eggplant, peeled and cubed
½ cup olive oil
1 large celery rib, chopped
1 green pepper, chopped
3 tablespoons chopped onion
2 tomatoes, chopped and drained
2½ tablespoons wine vinegar
1 tablespoon salt
1 tablespoon sugar
1 tablespoon capers
3 ounces tomato paste
Coarsely ground pepper
¼ cup sliced ripe olives
½ cup pitted green olives, chopped
Whole wheat pita bread

In large frying pan, saute eggplant in olive oil for 10 minutes. Remove eggplant with slotted spoon and drain. In remaining oil, saute celery, green pepper and onion until soft. Add eggplant, tomatoes, vinegar, salt, sugar, capers, tomato paste, pepper, ripe olives and green olives. Simmer for 15 minutes. To serve, split pita bread and cut into triangles. Bake at 350° until crisp. Serve with relish. *Relish may be prepared ahead and refrigerated for 2 weeks.*

Serves 12

Stuffed Snow Peas

Pretty as a picture

¼ pound fresh snow peas

6 ounces cream cheese, softened

¼ teaspoon garlic powder

¼ teaspoon Italian herb seasoning

2 tablespoons mayonnaise

Tabasco sauce to taste

String pea pods and remove peas, reserving ¼ cup. Set pods aside. Puree peas in blender. Add and puree the following ingredients until well blended: cream cheese, garlic powder, herb seasoning, mayonnaise and Tabasco sauce. Using pastry tube or spoon, fill pods with mixture and chill. *Must be prepared ahead.*

Serves 12

New Potato Skins

A sure bet

20 small new potatoes

Salt to taste

2 cups grated Cheddar cheese

3 ounces bacon bits

1 cup sour cream with chives

Boil potatoes in jackets until done. Drain, cool and halve. Scoop centers from potatoes, reserving pulp for another use. Salt shells, stuff with cheese and top with bacon bits. Bake at 350° until cheese is melted. Serve with sour cream. *May be prepared ahead. May be frozen.*

Serves 10

Cheesy Olive Squares

Tasty morsels best served warm

8 white bread slices, trimmed

2 cups grated Cheddar or Swiss cheese

2 tablespoons mayonnaise

Garlic salt to taste

1 cup chopped ripe olives

Toast and quarter bread. Set aside. Blend cheese, mayonnaise and garlic salt. Stir in olives. Spread on toast and broil until bubbly. *May be prepared ahead before assembling.*

Serves 12

Puffed Cheese Pastry

Purchased pastry makes this a breeze

4 bacon slices
4 ounces whipped cream cheese
1 egg
1 teaspoon lemon juice
1 teaspoon chopped chives
Pepper to taste
½ cup grated sharp white natural Cheddar cheese
1 (10x9 inch) frozen puff pastry sheet, thawed
Milk

Fry bacon, drain, crumble and set aside. With mixer, blend cream cheese, egg, lemon juice, chives and pepper. Stir in Cheddar cheese and bacon. Chill. Roll and cut pastry to yield 30 (2 inch) squares. Top each square with rounded teaspoon of filling and brush edges with milk. Fold to form triangle and seal edges with fork. Arrange on baking sheet and chill. Place in 450° oven and immediately reduce heat to 400°. Bake for 12 minutes or until brown. *Must be prepared ahead. May be refrigerated or frozen.*

Serves 10

Mexican Cheese Ball

This one has <u>authority</u>

1 tablespoon water
1 ounce onion dip mix
4 cups grated sharp Cheddar cheese
4 ounces canned chopped green chilies
2 ounces diced pimiento, drained
½ cup mayonnaise
4 tablespoons butter, softened
¼ to ½ teaspoon cayenne pepper
Paprika or cayenne pepper
Tortilla chips

In small bowl, mix water and onion dip mix. Set aside. In larger bowl, mix cheese, green chilies and pimiento. Add mayonnaise, butter and cayenne pepper and blend. Add onion dip mixture and mix well. Chill. Shape into ball and sprinkle with paprika or additional cayenne pepper. Serve with chips. *Must be prepared ahead. May be frozen.*

Serves 12

Deli Cheese Ball

Deserves space at your next party

16 ounces cream cheese, softened

1 teaspoon prepared horseradish

1 teaspoon Worcestershire sauce

½ teaspoon garlic salt

1 tablespoon mayonnaise

2½ ounces thinly sliced corned beef, finely chopped

½ cup chopped olives or pecans

Crackers

With mixer, blend cream cheese, horseradish, Worcestershire sauce, garlic salt and mayonnaise. Stir in corned beef and chill. Shape into ball and roll in olives or pecans. Serve with crackers. *Must be prepared ahead.*

Serves 12

Gourmet Cheese Balls

Flavor combination you can't beat

2 cups grated Gouda or Gruyere cheese

4 ounces feta cheese

8 ounces cream cheese, softened

1 teaspoon dill

¼ cup butter, melted

1 garlic clove, pressed

Salt to taste

Chopped nuts or parsley

Wheat crackers

Fresh fruit

With mixer, blend cheeses, dill, butter, garlic and salt. Halve and chill. Shape into 2 balls and roll in nuts or parsley. Serve with crackers and fruit. *Must be prepared ahead. May be frozen.*

Serves 24

Boursin Cheese Ball

For the thrifty gourmet

½ cup butter, softened
16 ounces cream cheese, softened
¾ ounce cheese garlic salad dressing mix
½ cup grated Parmesan cheese
Coarsely ground pepper
Crackers

With mixer, blend butter, cream cheese, salad dressing mix and Parmesan cheese. Freeze for at least 24 hours. Before serving, thaw, shape into ball and roll in pepper. Serve with crackers. *Must be prepared ahead. May be refrozen.*

Serves 12

Snappy Cheese Ball

Lively flavored, high powered

16 ounces cream cheese, softened
2½ cups grated Cheddar cheese
2 bunches green onions, chopped
2 tablespoons diced pimiento
1½ tablespoons Tabasco sauce
1½ tablespoons Worcestershire sauce
1 cup chopped nuts
Crackers

Blend cream cheese and Cheddar cheese. Add onions, pimiento, Tabasco sauce and Worcestershire sauce, mixing well. Halve and chill. Shape into 2 balls and roll in nuts. Serve with crackers. *Must be prepared ahead.*

Serves 24

Party Scramble

Fix in a minute and enjoy

4 teaspoons dill
¾ cup grated Parmesan cheese
1 teaspoon salt (optional)
1 cup butter
12 ounces Rice Chex cereal

In small bowl, mix dill, Parmesan cheese and salt. Set aside. Melt butter in large frying pan or stockpot. Add cereal and stir until lightly brown. Sprinkle with cheese mixture and gently stir. Serve as party snack. *May be prepared ahead. Keeps well.*

Serves 12

Party Snack Mix
For family and friends

3 cups small pretzels
2 cups shoestring potatoes
2 cups Spanish peanuts
1½ cups seasoned croutons
3 ounces canned French fried onion rings
½ cup butter, melted
½ cup grated Parmesan cheese

In large bowl, mix pretzels, shoestring potatoes, peanuts, croutons and onion rings. Pour butter over mixture, sprinkle with Parmesan cheese and mix well. Spread on 15x10 inch jelly roll pan or shallow roasting pan. Bake at 250° for 1 hour, stirring twice during cooking. *May be prepared ahead. Keeps well.*

Serves 12

Margaritas by the Gallon
Good to the last drop

12 ounces frozen lemonade concentrate, thawed
6 ounces frozen limeade concentrate, thawed
2 cups lime juice
1 cup Rose's lime juice
1 fifth tequila
12 ounces Triple Sec

Mix all ingredients in gallon jug. Add water to fill. Mix well and chill. *Must be prepared ahead.*

20 (6 ounce) servings

Bloody Marys by the Gallon
Guaranteed brunch winner

5 tablespoons celery salt
3 tablespoons pepper
2 tablespoons prepared horseradish
¼ cup Worcestershire sauce
½ cup lime juice
3 quarts tomato juice
1 fifth vodka
Celery ribs

Mix celery salt and pepper. Set aside. Mix horseradish, Worcestershire sauce and lime juice. In gallon container, add both mixtures, tomato juice and vodka, stirring well. Serve over ice and garnish with celery. *May be prepared ahead, omitting vodka, and refrigerated.*

16 (12 ounce) servings

Pina Amaretto Colada
A heavenly island drink

1½ ounces pina colada mix
1½ ounces Amaretto
1 cup ice
Fresh pineapple slice or cherry

In blender, mix pina colada mix, Amaretto and ice until slushy. Serve in cocktail glass and garnish with pineapple or cherry.

1 (8 ounce) serving

Pi Ti
Poolside refresher

12 ounces pineapple juice
2 ounces lime juice
4 ounces passion fruit juice
4 ounces light rum
4 ounces dark rum

Mix all ingredients in quart container. Fill with ice and stir to chill.

4 (8 ounce) servings

Rum Citrus Cooler

Bartender's secret from a well known hangout

1 ½ ounces rum
½ ounce Triple Sec
½ ounce lime juice
1 ½ ounces orange juice
½ ounce simple syrup
Lemon lime soft drink
Lemon or lime slice
Fresh mint

Mix rum, Triple Sec, lime juice, orange juice and simple syrup. Pour into tall glass over ice and top with splash of soft drink. Garnish with fruit slice or mint. *May be prepared ahead.*

1 (12 ounce) serving

Simple Syrup

1 part water
2 parts sugar

In saucepan, combine water and sugar and boil for 5 minutes. Cool.

Orange Blossoms

. . .hit the spot

6 ounces frozen orange juice concentrate
6 ounces milk
6 ounces vodka
2 egg whites
4 cups ice
Fresh mint

Mix orange juice, milk, vodka and egg whites in blender until frothy. Add ice and mix until crushed. Garnish with mint.

5 (8 ounce) servings

Grand Marnier Frappe

Guests will be impressed

1 tablespoon grated orange peel
1 cup orange juice
1 cup sugar
3 ounces Grand Marnier
3 cups orange juice

In blender, mix orange peel, 1 cup orange juice, sugar and Grand Marnier for 15 seconds. Mix in remaining orange juice. Pour into 2 ice cube trays and freeze. To serve, blend cubes, 1 tray at a time, for 30 seconds or until mixture is slushy. *Must be prepared ahead.*

6 (8 ounce) servings

Southern Mint Juleps

Omit the bourbon for your teetotalers

2½ cups sugar
2 cups water
¾ cup lemon juice
¾ cup orange juice
2 tablespoons grated orange peel
1 cup fresh mint
Ice water
Bourbon
Fresh mint

Boil sugar and water for 10 minutes and cool slightly. Mix lemon juice, orange juice, orange peel and mint in 2 quart glass jar. Mix in sugar water. Refrigerate for at least 24 hours. To serve, pour 4 tablespoons syrup mixture into tall glass, fill halfway with ice water and add bourbon and ice to fill. Garnish with mint. *Syrup mixture must be prepared ahead. Will keep for 2 weeks in refrigerator or may be frozen.*

12 (12 ounce) servings

Brandy Alexanders

Did I really have seconds

1 quart vanilla or chocolate chip ice cream
3 ounces cherry brandy
3 ounces white creme de cacao
½ cup milk
Nutmeg

In blender, add ice cream, brandy, creme de cacao and milk. Mix until smooth. Pour into champagne glass and sprinkle with nutmeg.

10 (4 ounce) servings

Colorado Bulldog

Tastes like an ice cream soda . . . Be careful

1½ ounces Kahlua
1½ ounces vodka
2 ounces milk
½ ounce cola

Pour Kahlua and vodka into tall glass. Fill with ice and stir in milk. Top with cola.

1 (12 ounce) serving

Holiday Eggnog

Make a week ahead and relax

4 eggs, separated
¾ cup brandy
2 tablespoons rum
2 cups whipping cream
¾ cup sugar
2 cups half and half

With mixer, beat egg whites until stiff and set aside. Beat egg yolks and stir in brandy, rum and whipping cream. Fold in egg whites. Add sugar and half and half, stirring well. Refrigerate for 1 week before serving. *Must be prepared ahead.*

12 (4 ounce) servings

Coffee Cordial

It's fun to taste and taste and taste . .

1 cup sugar

1 1/2 cups brown sugar

2 cups water

1/4 cup instant coffee granules

12 ounces vodka

3 tablespoons vanilla extract

Combine sugar, brown sugar and water in saucepan. Bring to a boil and simmer for 5 minutes. Remove from heat. Add coffee, stirring until dissolved. When cool, pour into 1 quart glass container. Mix in vodka and vanilla. Cover securely and store at room temperature for 2 weeks. *Must be prepared ahead.*

10 (3 ounce) servings

Vineyard Punch

Entertain with ease

1 cup water

3 cinnamon sticks

12 ounces frozen grape juice
    concentrate, thawed

12 ounces frozen grapefruit
    juice concentrate, thawed

1/2 cup lemon juice

2 cups California port wine

2 quarts ginger ale, chilled

Simmer water and cinnamon sticks for 5 minutes. Cool and strain. Pour into 2 quart container. Add juices and wine. Mix well and refrigerate for several hours. To serve, pour into large punch bowl and stir in ginger ale. *Must be prepared ahead.*

20 (4 ounce) servings

Champagne Punch

A sparkling party drink

2 cups sugar
2 cups water
¼ cup lemon juice
6 ounces frozen orange juice concentrate, thawed
1½ cups apple juice
2 cups pineapple juice
2 fifths champagne
3 cups ginger ale
Strawberries

In saucepan, bring sugar and water to a rapid boil and continue boiling for 1 minute. Set aside and cool. In punch bowl, mix juices. Add sugar mixture, stirring well. Mix in champagne, ginger ale and ice. Garnish with strawberries. *May be prepared ahead and frozen, omitting champagne, ginger ale and ice.*

50 (4 ounce) servings

Orange Smoothie

Athletes of all ages request seconds

6 ounces frozen orange juice concentrate
1½ cups water
½ cup milk
⅓ cup sugar
1 teaspoon vanilla extract
2 cups ice
1 cup vanilla ice cream (optional)

Mix all ingredients in blender for 30 seconds.

4 (12 ounce) servings

Valentine Punch

Cupid's choice

1 quart cranberry juice cocktail
2 cups pineapple juice
1 ½ cups sugar
2 quarts ginger ale
Light rum (optional)

Mix juices with sugar. Chill. Add ginger ale and rum at serving time.

30 (4 ounce) servings

Autumn Cider

Hot and spicy

1 gallon apple cider
12 ounces frozen orange juice concentrate
¼ cup brown sugar
3 cups water
Cinnamon sticks

Combine cider, orange juice, brown sugar and water in stockpot, stirring well. Heat until steaming but not boiling. Serve in mugs and garnish with cinnamon sticks. *May be prepared ahead.*

12 (12 ounce) servings

Hot Cranberry Tea

Delightful aroma puts you in a holiday mood

2 cups sugar
4 cinnamon sticks
2 cups water
2 quarts cranberry juice cocktail
2 cups orange juice
3 tablespoons lemon juice
4 cups water
4 cinnamon sticks
Additional cinnamon sticks

In stockpot, bring sugar, 4 cinnamon sticks and 2 cups water to a boil. Add juices and stir in remaining 4 cups water and 4 cinnamon sticks. Simmer until steaming but not boiling. Garnish with additional cinnamon sticks. *May be prepared ahead.*

16 (8 ounce) servings

Iced Tea Punch

Economical party pleaser

1 quart water
2 fresh mint sprigs
8 small tea bags
1 cup sugar
6 ounces frozen limeade concentrate, thawed
6 ounces frozen lemonade concentrate, thawed

In large saucepan, bring 1 quart water to a boil then add mint and tea bags. Cover and steep for 30 minutes. In gallon jar, mix sugar, limeade and lemonade. Pour in hot tea mixture and add water to fill. Serve in tall glass over ice. *May be prepared ahead.*

20 (12 ounce) servings

Tea Sippers

Delightful on a warm afternoon

1 cup sugar
1 cup strong hot tea
⅓ cup lemon juice
¾ cup orange juice
2 cups ginger ale
2 cups club soda
Orange slices

In 1 quart container, dissolve sugar in tea. Stir in juices. To serve, pour into punch bowl over ice. Mix in ginger ale and club soda. Garnish with orange slices.

10 (12 ounce) servings

Souper favorites from first course to main course

Cold Strawberry Soup
Superb summer choice

1 ½ cups strawberry preserves

1 ¼ cups sour cream

¾ cup half and half or yogurt

⅔ cup sherry or kirsch

1 ½ tablespoons grenadine

1 pint fresh strawberries, halved

Fresh mint

In large bowl, whisk preserves with sour cream. Stir in half and half, sherry and grenadine. Cover and refrigerate for several hours. Just before serving, fold in strawberries. Garnish with mint. *Must be prepared ahead.*

Serves 6

Chilled Cantaloupe Soup
Great presentation

6 cantaloupes

¾ cup dry sherry

¾ cup sugar

1 ½ cups orange juice

Fresh mint

Halve cantaloupes, cutting across ribs, and remove seeds. Scoop pulp from cantaloupe halves, leaving ½ inch thick shells and reserving pulp. Set shells aside. In blender combine pulp, sherry, sugar and orange juice. Mix until smooth. Chill. To serve, cut thin slice from bottom of each shell, being careful not to puncture shell. Fill with soup and garnish with mint. *Must be prepared ahead.*

Serves 12

Chilled Spinach Soup

Refreshing in the hot summer

1 tablespoon minced onion
2 tablespoons butter
2 tablespoons flour
1 quart milk
Salt to taste
Pepper to taste
Nutmeg to taste
Paprika to taste
10 ounces frozen chopped spinach, cooked and drained
½ to 1 cup grated Parmesan cheese
Croutons

In stockpot, saute onion in butter. Blend in flour. Gradually add milk and stir until thickened. Mix in salt, pepper, nutmeg, paprika, spinach and Parmesan cheese. Chill. Serve with croutons. *Must be prepared ahead.*

Serves 6

Zucchini Soup

Hot or cold. . .swell eating

1 zucchini, chopped
1 onion, chopped
½ teaspoon curry powder
2½ cups chicken broth
1 cup sour cream
Salt to taste
Pepper to taste

In saucepan, gently boil zucchini, onion, curry powder and chicken broth until zucchini and onion are tender. Transfer to blender. Puree with sour cream, salt and pepper. Serve hot or cold. *May be prepared ahead.*

Serves 6

Crab Bisque

Nice to serve in mugs

8 ounces fresh or frozen crabmeat

20 ounces cream of mushroom soup

20 ounces cream of asparagus soup

2 cups half and half

2⅔ cups milk

1 teaspoon Worcestershire sauce

½ teaspoon salt

¾ cup sherry

Blend crabmeat with soups, cover and refrigerate overnight. In saucepan, mix crabmeat mixture, half and half, milk, Worcestershire sauce, salt and sherry. Heat and serve in mugs. *Must be prepared ahead.*

Serves 10

Curried Tomato Bisque

We bet you'll want to double this recipe

4 green onions, minced

2 tablepoons butter

20 ounces tomato soup

2½ cups water

½ to ¾ tablespoon curry powder

2 teaspoons lime juice

Sour cream (optional)

Lime slices (optional)

Hard boiled egg slices (optional)

In large saucepan, saute onions in butter. Add soup and water, mixing well. Stir in curry powder then lime juice. May be garnished with sour cream or lime or egg slices. *May be prepared ahead.*

Serves 6

Mushroom Bisque

Easier than you think

40 ounces cream of mushroom soup

2 cups half and half

2 cups milk

1 cup sour cream

2 cups grated Velveeta cheese

⅛ teaspoon cayenne pepper

1 pound fresh mushrooms, sliced

¼ cup dry white wine

In stockpot, mix soup, half and half, milk, sour cream, cheese and cayenne pepper. Cook over medium low heat until cheese is melted, stirring frequently. Add mushrooms and cook over low heat for 20 to 30 minutes, stirring frequently. Stir in wine just before serving. *May be prepared ahead.*

Serves 6

Hearty Vegetable Soup

Cold weather warmer

2 bunches green onions, chopped

1 celery rib, chopped

½ cup butter

5 cups chicken broth

5 chicken bouillon cubes

6 ounces non dairy coffee creamer

2 to 3 carrots, sliced

2 potatoes, sliced

¼ cup uncooked rice

10 ounces frozen chopped asparagus

10 ounces frozen chopped spinach

Grated Parmesan cheese

Saute onions and celery in butter until tender. Set aside. In stockpot, bring chicken broth and bouillon cubes to a boil. Whisk in non dairy creamer, onions, and celery. Mix in carrots, potatoes and rice. Cook for 45 minutes over low heat. Add asparagus and spinach, cooking for 1 hour. Sprinkle with Parmesan cheese. *May be prepared ahead.*

Serves 8

Kitchen Sink Soup

It's all here

1 pound ground chuck
2 large onions, chopped
1 potato, coarsely chopped
2 carrots, coarsely chopped
1 celery rib, coarsely chopped
1 cup shredded cabbage
20 ounces canned whole tomatoes
¼ cup uncooked rice
1 bay leaf, crushed
½ teaspoon thyme
¼ teaspoon basil
1 tablespoon salt
Pepper to taste
1½ quarts water

In stockpot, brown chuck with onions. Pour off grease. Mix in potato, carrots, celery, cabbage, tomatoes, rice, bay leaf, thyme, basil, salt, pepper and water. Bring to a boil, cover and simmer for 1 to 1½ hours. *May be prepared ahead. May be frozen.*

Serves 6

Barbecued Bean Soup

Substantial and filling

1 pound dried navy beans
2½ quarts water
2 tablespoons oil for frying
2 pounds beef short ribs
2 tablespoons flour
1 small onion, chopped
1 tablespoon salt
¼ teaspoon pepper
¾ cup barbecue sauce

In stockpot, heat beans and water to boiling and boil for 2 minutes. Remove from heat, cover and let stand for 1 hour. Heat oil in frying pan. Coat ribs with flour. Brown on all sides in hot oil. Reserving drippings in frying pan, add ribs to beans. Saute onion in drippings for 5 minutes. To beans and ribs, mix in onion, drippings, salt and pepper. Bring to a boil, reduce heat and simmer for 2½ hours or until meat is tender. Remove ribs and cool slightly. Cut meat from bones, dice and return to soup. Stir in barbecue sauce and heat thoroughly. *May be prepared ahead. May be frozen.*

Serves 10

Corn Chowder
Warms you in the winter

2 potatoes, peeled and coarsely chopped
1 large onion, thinly sliced
1 cup water
½ teaspoon salt
1 quart milk
17 ounces canned cream style corn
17 ounces canned whole kernel corn
4 tablespoons butter
Salt to taste
Pepper to taste

In stockpot, mix potatoes, onion, water and salt. Cook for 20 minutes or until potatoes are tender. Stir in milk, cream style corn, whole kernel corn, butter, salt and pepper. Heat but do not boil. *May be prepared ahead.*

Serves 8

Tortilla Soup
Entertain a group with ease

60 ounces chicken with rice soup
1 cup red wine
28 ounces stewed tomatoes
6 celery ribs, chopped
½ teaspoon crushed mint
1 quart water
6 chicken bouillon cubes
2 large onions, chopped
2 teaspoons sugar
Tortilla chips
Grated Monterey Jack cheese

Mix soup, wine, tomatoes, celery, mint, water, bouillon cubes, onions and sugar in stockpot. Simmer for 1 hour. Line serving bowls with chips, pour in soup and sprinkle with cheese. *May be prepared ahead. May be frozen.*

Serves 10

Split Pea Soup

Soul food

¼ pound bacon, coarsely chopped
2 pounds dried split peas
2¾ quarts water
1 cup chicken broth
2 onions, quartered
1 garlic clove
2 carrots, sliced
1 celery rib, sliced
3 parsley sprigs
2 bay leaves
1 smoked ham shank
Salt to taste
Pepper to taste
Cayenne pepper to taste
½ teaspoon garlic powder
2 cups half and half
1½ cups milk
4 to 6 frankfurters or smoked sausage, sliced

Fry bacon, drain and set aside. In stockpot, mix peas, water, chicken broth, bacon, onions, garlic, carrots, celery, parsley, bay leaves and ham. Bring to a boil and simmer for 3 hours, stirring often. Remove and discard celery, parsley, bay leaves and garlic. Remove and puree onions and carrots then return to soup. Remove ham. Cut meat into bite size pieces and return to soup. Add salt, pepper, cayenne pepper, garlic powder, half and half, milk and sausage. Simmer for 30 minutes, stirring frequently. *May be prepared ahead. May be frozen.*

Serves 10

French Onion Soup

An epicurean's choice

6 bacon slices
6 onions, sliced
Salt to taste
2½ cups beef broth
4 cups water
6 French bread slices
Freshly grated Parmesan or mozzarella cheese

In stockpot, fry bacon, drain and crumble, reserving drippings. Saute onions in drippings. Mix in salt, beef broth and water. Simmer for 1 hour. To serve, place 1 slice French bread in broiler proof soup bowl. Sprinkle with bacon. Fill with soup and top with cheese. Broil until bubbly and lightly brown. *Soup may be prepared ahead.*

Serves 6

Fresh Mushroom Soup

A rich and creamy luxury

1 pound fresh mushrooms, sliced

4 tablespoons butter

4 cups whipping cream

4 cups chicken broth

2 egg yolks

2 tablespoons lemon juice

1/4 cup sherry

Salt to taste

Pepper to taste

Croutons

In stockpot, saute mushrooms in butter until tender. Slowly stir in cream. Reduce heat, cover and simmer for 10 minutes. Mix in chicken broth. Beat egg yolks with lemon juice and stir slowly into soup. Heat but do not boil. Stir in sherry, salt and pepper. Garnish with croutons.

Serves 8

Wild Rice Soup

From Minnesota. . .the wild rice capital

1 onion, minced

1/2 pound fresh mushrooms, sliced

1 large celery rib, thinly sliced

4 tablespoons butter

1/2 cup flour

6 cups chicken broth

4 cups cooked wild rice

1/2 teaspoon salt

1/2 teaspoon curry powder

1/4 teaspoon pepper

1/2 teaspoon chervil

2 1/2 cups half and half

2/3 cup dry sherry

Parsley or chives

In stockpot, saute onion, mushrooms and celery in butter for 3 minutes. Stir in flour, and gradually add chicken broth. Stir continuously for 5 minutes or until mixture is slightly thickened. Stir in rice, salt, curry powder, pepper and chervil. Reduce heat to low and mix in half and half and sherry. Simmer for 10 minutes, stirring occasionally. Garnish with parsley or chives. *May be prepared ahead.*

Serves 10

Fresh Tomato Soup

Piquant flavored and deserves encores

4 chicken bouillon cubes
2 quarts water
5 bacon slices
2 tablespoons butter
2 tablespoons olive oil
3 tablespoons flour
4 garlic cloves, thinly sliced
2 carrots, finely chopped
¾ cup minced onion
2 teaspoons sugar
1 cup white wine
4 tablespoons tomato paste
10 tomatoes, finely chopped
¼ teaspoon thyme
¼ teaspoon tarragon
¼ teaspoon basil
1 teaspoon salt
¼ teaspoon pepper

In stockpot, boil bouillon cubes in water until dissolved. Set aside. Cook bacon in large frying pan. Reserving drippings, drain bacon, crumble and set aside. Blend butter, oil and flour in drippings. Cook over medium heat until bubbly. Mix in garlic, carrots and onion, cooking for 5 minutes. Stir in sugar, wine, tomato paste and tomatoes. Combine in stockpot with bouillon. Stir in thyme, tarragon, basil, salt and pepper. Cook over low heat for 1 hour. Sprinkle with bacon. *May be prepared ahead.*

Serves 8

Pork and Bean Salad

Dynamic duo

16 ounces canned pork and beans, drained
1 large onion, chopped
1 small tomato, chopped
¼ cup chopped sweet pickles
Salt to taste
Pepper to taste

Mix all ingredients in medium bowl. Cover and refrigerate until ready to serve. *Must be prepared ahead. Will keep for 2 to 3 days.*

Serves 4

Chili Spiced Beans

Great for tailgate parties

15 ounces canned red kidney beans	In large colander, add beans. Rinse with water and drain well. Transfer to large bowl and mix with corn, green onions, parsley, celery and green chilies. Pour dressing over vegetables and toss. Cover and refrigerate for at least 6 hours, stirring frequently. *Must be prepared ahead.*

15 ounces canned red kidney beans

16 ounces canned pinto beans

16 ounces canned Garbanzo beans

17 ounces canned whole kernel corn, drained

6 green onions, chopped

¼ cup snipped parsley

2 celery ribs, sliced

4 ounces canned chopped green chilies

In large colander, add beans. Rinse with water and drain well. Transfer to large bowl and mix with corn, green onions, parsley, celery and green chilies. Pour dressing over vegetables and toss. Cover and refrigerate for at least 6 hours, stirring frequently. *Must be prepared ahead.*

Serves 12

Dressing

¾ cup olive oil or salad oil

¼ cup wine vinegar

1 garlic clove, minced

½ tablespoon salt

1 teaspoon chili powder

1 teaspoon oregano

¼ teaspoon cumin

⅛ teaspoon Tabasco sauce

Mix all ingredients well.

Chinese Slaw

Better the next day

14 ounces canned bean sprouts, drained
16 ounces canned seasoned green beans, drained
8 ounces sliced water chestnuts, drained
17 ounces canned small green peas, drained
3 celery ribs, chopped
1 onion, thinly sliced
1 cup sugar
¾ cup wine vinegar
½ cup salad oil
Salt to taste
Pepper to taste

In large bowl, mix bean sprouts, green beans, water chestnuts, peas, celery and onion. In separate bowl, combine sugar, vinegar, oil, salt and pepper, mixing well. Pour over vegetables and chill. *Must be prepared ahead.*

Serves 10

Sauerkraut Salad

A different summer salad

28 ounces canned sauerkraut, drained
1 onion, coarsely chopped
1 green pepper, coarsely chopped
1 tablespoon diced pimiento
¾ cup water
⅔ cup vinegar
1 cup sugar
½ cup salad oil

Mix sauerkraut, onion, green pepper and pimiento. Set aside. In saucepan, heat water and vinegar. Stir in sugar until dissolved. Add oil, mixing well. Pour over salad. Cover and refrigerate overnight. *Must be prepared ahead.*

Serves 6

Avocado with Dressing
Fancy luncheon salad

3 tablespoons butter
3 tablespoons catsup
2 tablespoons water
2 tablespoons vinegar
2 tablespoons sugar
2 tablespoons Worcestershire sauce
½ teaspoon salt
Tabasco sauce to taste
2 avocados, halved and peeled

Combine butter, catsup, water, vinegar, sugar, Worcestershire sauce, salt and Tabasco sauce in saucepan. Heat and stir until thoroughly blended. Pour over avocado halves. *Sauce may be prepared ahead.*

Serves 4

Harvest Vegetable Marinade
Updated family favorite

12 ounces canned whole kernel white corn, drained
16 ounces canned French style green beans, drained
1 large green pepper, chopped
1 large red onion, chopped
4 celery ribs, chopped
32 ounces canned small green peas, drained

Mix corn, green beans, green pepper, onion and celery. Gently stir in peas. Pour dressing over vegetables and lightly stir. May be served hot or cold. *Must be prepared ahead if served cold.*

Serves 12

Dressing

1 cup sugar
¾ cup vinegar
½ cup salad oil
½ tablespoon salt
Garlic powder to taste

In small saucepan, mix all ingredients. Heat and stir until sugar dissolves.

Cauliflower Medley
For summer outings

1 head cauliflower, separated into flowerets
2 celery ribs, chopped
1 green pepper, chopped
2 ounces diced pimiento, drained
¾ cup sliced stuffed green olives
3 tablespoons olive juice
8 ounces Cheddar cheese, cubed
8 ounces Caesar salad dressing
1 cup sour cream

In large bowl, mix all ingredients. Cover and refrigerate overnight. *Must be prepared ahead.*

Serves 8

Marinated Vegetables
Fine, fresh flavor

2 pounds fresh mushrooms, sliced
2 bunches broccoli, separated into flowerets
2 pints cherry tomatoes

Mix all ingredients. Toss with dressing, cover and refrigerate overnight. *Must be prepared ahead.*

Serves 12

Dressing

1 teaspoon sugar
1 teaspoon ginger
1 tablespoon tarragon
2 tablespoons red wine vinegar
8 ounces Italian salad dressing

Mix all ingredients.

Garden Bouquet Salad

Double duty salad and vegetable

10 ounces frozen broccoli spears

9 ounces frozen French style green beans

10 ounces frozen asparagus spears

10 ounces frozen artichoke hearts

1 green pepper, chopped

1 cucumber, peeled and sliced

Dressing

½ cup half and half

2 tablespoons lemon juice

2 tablespoons garlic vinegar

1 cup mayonnaise

¾ cup snipped parsley

1 onion, minced

2 tablespoons anchovy paste

Using ½ the cooking time, separately prepare broccoli, green beans, asparagus and artichokes according to package directions. Cut into bite size pieces and cool. Mix in green pepper and cucumber. Pour dressing over vegetables and toss. Cover and chill. *Must be prepared ahead.*

Serves 18

Mix all ingredients.

New Potato Salad

Blue ribbon

4 pounds new potatoes

1½ ounces Italian salad dressing mix, prepared

2 bunches green onions with tops, minced

2 cups snipped parsley

1 cup mayonnaise

Salt to taste

Pepper to taste

Boil potatoes in jackets until done then drain. While still warm, cut potatoes into bite size pieces. Mix with dressing in large bowl, cover and refrigerate overnight. Mix potatoes, green onions, parsley, mayonnaise, salt and pepper. Serve at room temperature. *Must be prepared ahead.*

Serves 12

Gentlemen's Potato Salad

For his pleasure

10 potatoes
2 cups mayonnaise
1 cup whipping cream
¼ cup vinegar
1 bunch green onions, chopped
1 large onion, chopped
1 tablespoon celery seed
1 teaspoon garlic salt
Seasoned salt to taste

Boil potatoes in jackets until done. Cool, peel and cube. Prepare dressing by blending mayonnaise, whipping cream, vinegar, onions, celery seed, garlic salt and seasoned salt. Fold dressing into potatoes, cover and chill. *Must be prepared ahead.*

Serves 12

Fourth of July Potato Salad

America's favorite

6 large potatoes
4 to 5 eggs, hard boiled and coarsely chopped
4 celery ribs, coarsely chopped
3 tablespoons chopped onion
4 tablespoons sweet relish
Salt to taste
1 cup salad dressing
1 cup sour cream
1 tablespoon vinegar
1 to 2 tablespoons sugar
1 tablespoon prepared mustard
1 tablespoon celery seed
Paprika

Boil potatoes in jackets until done and drain. Cool, peel and cube. Mix with eggs, celery, onion, relish and salt. Set aside. In separate bowl, blend salad dressing, sour cream, vinegar, sugar, mustard and celery seed. Pour over potatoes and mix thoroughly. Cover and refrigerate for 24 hours. Sprinkle with paprika before serving. *Must be prepared ahead.*

Serves 8

Garden Salad Bowl

Beautiful salad you'll love to serve

*¾ pound fresh spinach, torn
    into pieces*

*1 stalk red leaf lettuce, torn
    into pieces*

*3 eggs, hard boiled and
    chopped*

*½ head cauliflower, separated
    into flowerets*

*2 small avocados, coarsely
    chopped*

1 cup fresh bean sprouts

*4 bacon slices, cooked, drained
    and crumbled*

*1 bunch green onions with tops,
    chopped*

Toss all ingredients. Add salad dressing and toss again. *Dressing must be prepared ahead and will keep for several days.*

Serves 10

Dressing

1 cup salad oil

1 onion, chopped

1 teaspoon Worcestershire sauce

⅓ cup catsup

½ cup vinegar

¾ cup sugar

2 teaspoons salt

Pepper to taste

Mix all ingredients, cover and chill.

Caesar Salad

Entertain your guests with a flair

3 large heads Romaine lettuce, torn into pieces

½ cup salad oil

Croutons

Grated Romano cheese

Toss lettuce with salad dressing. Add oil and toss again. Garnish with croutons and Romano cheese.

Serves 8

Dressing

2 garlic cloves, pressed

1 tablespoon Worcestershire sauce

¾ teaspoon salt

½ teaspoon cracked pepper

⅓ cup lemon juice

1 egg, room temperature

Whisk all ingredients.

Wilted Lettuce

All generations will remember this one

1 head lettuce, torn into pieces

1 egg, hard boiled and sliced

3 to 5 green onions, chopped

Toss all ingredients. Add warm dressing and lightly toss.

Serves 6

Dressing

2 tablespoons bacon drippings

¼ cup plus ¾ teaspoon vinegar

½ teaspoon salt

½ tablespoon sugar

3 tablespoons water

Mix all ingredients in small saucepan and bring to a boil. Serve immediately.

Mandarin Orange Toss

Popular restaurant version. . .great with crepes

8 ounces canned mandarin oranges, drained

½ head lettuce, torn into pieces

2 celery ribs, chopped

1 tablespoon parsley flakes

2 tablespoons chopped chives

¼ cup slivered almonds, toasted

Add all ingredients and gently toss. Add salad dressing and toss again. *Dressing must be prepared ahead.*

Serves 6

Dressing

½ cup salad oil

½ teaspoon Tabasco sauce

1 tablespoon salt

¼ cup sugar

¼ cup tarragon vinegar

In container, mix all ingredients well. Refrigerate for several hours.

Italian Chicken Salad

Unforgettable

12 ounces marinated artichoke hearts

1 fryer, cooked, boned and chopped

8 ounces chicken flavored rice mix, prepared

4 green onions, chopped

½ cup chopped green pepper

1½ cups chopped ripe olives, drained

⅓ cup mayonnaise

Reserving liquid, drain and chop artichokes. In large bowl, mix with chicken, rice, onions, green pepper and olives. Set aside. Blend artichoke liquid with mayonnaise. Pour over salad and gently toss. Cover and refrigerate overnight. *Must be prepared ahead.*

Serves 8

Vienna Chicken Salad

Finally, a chicken salad for men

¼ cup tarragon vinegar
1 small onion, minced
1 tablespoon capers
1 teaspoon Dijon mustard
2 cups chopped cooked chicken breast
½ cup mayonnaise
¼ cup sour cream
Salt to taste
Pepper to taste
Crumbled bacon

In large bowl, mix vinegar, onion, capers and mustard. Add chicken, mixing well. Cover and refrigerate for several hours. Blend mayonnaise, sour cream, salt and pepper. Mix with chicken. Garnish with bacon. May also be used as sandwich filling. *Must be prepared ahead.*

Serves 4

Hawaiian Chicken Salad

New twist for basic recipe

4 cups chopped cooked chicken breast
3 celery ribs, coarsely chopped
⅔ cup seedless green grapes, halved
⅓ cup canned coconut
⅔ cup slivered almonds, toasted
¼ cup whipping cream, whipped
½ cup mayonnaise
1 tablespoon lemon juice
½ teaspoon salt

In large bowl, combine chicken, celery, grapes, coconut and almonds. Toss, mixing well. Blend whipped cream with mayonnaise, lemon juice and salt. Fold into chicken mixture. *May be prepared ahead and refrigerated.*

Serves 6

69

Avocado Chicken Salad

Lively and snappy

---

1 ½ cups chopped cooked chicken

½ cup mayonnaise

1 large celery rib, finely chopped

1 jalapeno pepper, finely chopped

1 tablespoon minced onion

1 tablespoon finely chopped carrots

1 tablespoon snipped parsley

Salt to taste

Coarsely ground pepper to taste

4 avocados, halved

Tortilla chips

Cherry tomatoes

Pitted olives

Dressing

---

1 cup mayonnaise

1 cup sour cream

2 tablespoons chopped cilantro or coriander

½ teaspoon cumin

Mix chicken, mayonnaise, celery, jalapeno pepper, onion, carrots, parsley, salt and pepper. Fill avocado halves and top with dressing. Garnish with tortilla chips, cherry tomatoes and olives. *Filling may be prepared ahead.*

Serves 8

Blend all ingredients.

Ham and Chicken Salad

Mandarin oranges add excitement

1½ cups cubed cooked ham

1 cup chopped cooked chicken

22 ounces canned mandarin oranges, drained

⅔ cup seedless green grapes, halved

1 celery rib, sliced

½ cup mayonnaise

½ cup salad dressing

¼ cup sour cream

Tabasco sauce to taste

¼ teaspoon Worcestershire sauce

½ teaspoon blue cheese salad dressing

½ teaspoon curry powder

Almonds

Coconut

Mix ham, chicken, oranges, grapes and celery in large bowl and set aside. Blend mayonnaise, salad dressing, sour cream, Tabasco sauce, Worcestershire sauce, blue cheese dressing and curry powder. Toss with salad. Cover and refrigerate for at least 12 hours. Garnish with almonds and coconut. *Must be prepared ahead.*

Serves 8

Taco Salad with Avocado Dressing
Texas favorite revised

1 pound ground beef
10 ounces canned tomatoes and green chilies
½ teaspoon garlic powder
1 teaspoon salt
1 teaspoon chili powder
1 head lettuce, torn into pieces
3 tomatoes, chopped
2 cups grated Cheddar cheese
3 green onions with tops, chopped
Sliced ripe olives
Crushed tortilla chips

In large frying pan, brown meat and pour off grease. Mix in tomatoes and green chilies, garlic powder, salt and chili powder. Simmer for 10 minutes. To serve, layer lettuce, meat, tomatoes, cheese, green onions, olives and chips. Top with Avocado Dressing.

Serves 6

Avocado Dressing

2 avocados, mashed
2 tablespoons lemon juice
1 cup sour cream
⅔ cup salad oil
1 teaspoon sugar
1 teaspoon garlic salt
1 teaspoon chili powder

Combine all ingredients, blending until smooth.

Chinese Crab Salad

Complements charcoal flavored meat

1 head lettuce, torn into pieces

2 celery ribs, diagonally sliced

4 green onions, chopped

*6 ounces fresh or frozen
    crabmeat*

*2 cups canned chow mein
    noodles*

Mix all ingredients and toss with dressing. *Dressing must be prepared ahead.*

Serves 6

Dressing

2 tablespoons sugar

1 teaspoon Accent

½ cup salad oil

1 teaspoon sesame oil

1 teaspoon salt

3 tablespoons wine vinegar

½ garlic clove, pressed

Mix all ingredients and chill.

Oriental Tuna Salad

Confuscius say. . .Happy to eat this tuna. Sorry, Charlie

*9 ounces frozen French style
    green beans, cooked and
    drained*

7 ounces canned tuna, drained

3 celery ribs, thinly sliced

½ cup mayonnaise

1 tablespoon lemon juice

½ tablespoon soy sauce

Garlic powder to taste

*1 cup canned chow mein
    noodles*

In bowl, mix beans with tuna, celery, mayonnaise, lemon juice, soy sauce and garlic powder. Cover and chill. Mix in noodles just before serving. *Must be prepared ahead.*

Serves 4

73

Confetti Rice Salad
Toss, chill and serve

**6 ounces long grain and wild
   rice, prepared**

¼ cup salad oil

2 tablespoons lemon juice

**¼ cup coarsely chopped
   cucumber**

**¼ cup coarsely chopped green
   pepper**

**1 green onion with top, thinly
   sliced**

1 tablespoon snipped parsley

1 tomato, coarsely chopped

Place rice in large bowl, cover and chill. Stir in oil, lemon juice, cucumber, green pepper, onion and parsley. Cover and refrigerate for 1 hour. Fold in tomatoes just before serving. *Must be prepared ahead.*

Serves 6

Cold Pasta Salad
Good on a hot day

1½ cups vinegar

1½ cups sugar

¼ cup salad oil

1 teaspoon garlic powder

2 tablespoons parsley flakes

2 tablespoons prepared mustard

1 teaspoon salt

½ teaspoon pepper

**1 pound Mostaccioli macaroni,
   cooked and drained**

3 celery ribs, finely chopped

1 cucumber, finely chopped

1 onion, minced

**¼ cup finely chopped green
   pepper**

In small saucepan, add vinegar, sugar and oil. Heat and stir until sugar dissolves. Remove from heat and cool. Add garlic powder, parsley flakes, mustard, salt and pepper, mixing well. Stir into macaroni, celery, cucumber, onion and green pepper. Cover and refrigerate for several hours. *Must be prepared ahead.*

Serves 8

Spaghetti Salad
Great with deli sandwiches

12 ounces vermicelli
3 tablespoons Accent
3 tablespoons lemon juice
½ cup salad oil
1 cup chopped ripe olives
4 ounces diced pimiento
½ cup mayonnaise
1 bunch green onions with tops, chopped

Break vermicelli into pieces, cook according to package directions and drain. Mix with Accent, lemon juice and oil. Cover and refrigerate overnight, stirring occasionally. Add olives, pimiento, mayonnaise and onions. Mix well and refrigerate for several hours. *Must be prepared ahead.*

Serves 12

Chicken Pasta Salad
Italian influence

12 ounces spaghetti, cooked and drained
28 ounces stewed tomatoes, drained and chopped
⅓ cup chopped ripe olives
1 bunch green onions, chopped
1 teaspoon salt
⅓ to ½ cup grated Parmesan cheese
2 cups chopped cooked chicken
1½ ounces Italian salad dressing mix, prepared

In large bowl, mix spaghetti, tomatoes, olives, onions, salt, Parmesan cheese and chicken. Add Italian dressing, tossing well. Cover and refrigerate overnight, stirring occasionally. *Must be prepared ahead.*

Serves 8

Pepperoni Pasta Salad

True to its name

12 ounces macaroni shells, cooked and drained

1 pound pepperoni, chopped

1 cup chopped ripe olives

1 cup pitted green olives, chopped

1 green pepper, chopped

3 celery ribs, chopped

1 small onion, chopped

3 tomatoes, seeded and chopped

1½ cups grated provolone cheese

Dressing

¾ cup salad oil

½ cup wine vinegar

1 teaspoon salt

1 teaspoon pepper

1 teaspoon sugar

½ teaspoon oregano

Mix pasta, pepperoni, ripe olives, green olives, green pepper, celery, onion and tomatoes. Cover and refrigerate for 24 hours. To serve, mix salad with dressing and cheese. *Must be prepared ahead.*

Serves 10

Mix all ingredients. Cover and refrigerate for 48 hours.

Paper Cup Frozen Salad

Easy enough for children to make

2 cups sour cream
2 tablespoons lemon juice
½ cup sugar
⅛ teaspoon salt
8 ounces canned crushed pineapple, drained
1 banana, chopped
Red food coloring
¼ cup chopped pecans
16 ounces pitted Bing cherries, drained

Blend sour cream, lemon juice, sugar, salt, pineapple, banana and enough red food coloring for pink tint. Fold in pecans and cherries. Spoon into paper lined muffin tin cups. Cover and freeze. Remove from freezer 15 minutes before serving. *Must be prepared ahead.*

Serves 12

Frozen Fruit Salad

A glamorous treat from the freezer

½ cup pitted Bing cherries, drained, reserving juice
32 large marshmallows
1 cup mayonnaise
2 cups ginger ale
12 ounces canned crushed pineapple, drained
16 ounces canned sliced peaches, drained
½ cup whipping cream, whipped

In large saucepan, slowly heat 2 tablespoons cherry juice and marshmallows, folding until marshmallows are ½ melted. Remove from heat and continue folding until smooth and fluffy. Place saucepan in water to cool. Blend in mayonnaise and gradually stir in ginger ale. Fold in cherries, pineapple, peaches and whipped cream. Freeze in tube pan. *Must be prepared ahead.*

Serves 20

Cherry Cola Salad
Try this one as a dessert also

6 ounces cherry gelatin
⅓ cup sugar
½ cup water
21 ounces cherry pie filling
¾ cup cola
1 cup chopped nuts
8 ounces canned crushed pineapple, drained, reserving juice

In saucepan, mix gelatin and sugar in water and boil gently over low heat for 5 minutes or until completely dissolved. Cool slightly. Add pie filling, cola, nuts and pineapple, mixing well. Pour into 13x9 inch dish and refrigerate until set. Spread on topping and chill. *Must be prepared ahead.*

Serves 10

Topping

½ cup sugar
½ cup reserved pineapple juice
1 egg, beaten
2 tablespoons cornstarch
2 tablespoons butter
3 ounces cream cheese, softened
8 ounces frozen whipped topping, thawed

Mix sugar, pineapple juice, egg, cornstarch and butter in saucepan. Cook over low heat until thickened. Blend in cream cheese. Cool and fold in whipped topping.

Orange Surprise
Find what's different

20 ounces canned crushed pineapple
¼ cup sugar
6 ounces orange gelatin
2 cups water
8 ounces frozen whipped topping, thawed
1 cup finely chopped nuts
1 cup grated Cheddar cheese

In saucepan, bring pineapple and sugar to a boil. Stir in gelatin until dissolved and mix in water. Refrigerate in large bowl until partially congealed. Fold in whipped topping, nuts and cheese. Pour into greased 8 cup mold and refrigerate until set. *Must be prepared ahead.*

Serves 12

Cranberry Eggnog Layered Salad
A holiday joy

First Layer

3 ounces lemon gelatin

1 cup boiling water

1 cup eggnog

¼ teaspoon rum extract

In bowl, dissolve lemon gelatin in water and cool to room temperature. Mix in eggnog and rum extract. Pour into greased 6 to 8 cup salad mold and refrigerate until partially congealed.

Serves 10

Second Layer

3 ounces raspberry gelatin

1 cup boiling water

½ teaspoon grated orange peel

14 ounces cranberry orange sauce

11 ounces canned mandarin oranges, drained

8 ounces canned crushed pineapple, drained

1 cup chopped nuts

In bowl, dissolve raspberry gelatin in water and cool to room temperature. Mix in orange peel, cranberry orange sauce, mandarin oranges, pineapple and nuts. Spoon onto first layer. Refrigerate until set. *Must be prepared ahead.*

Congealed Avocado Salad
A must for a fancy mold

3 ounces lemon gelatin

1 cup boiling water

2 large avocados, cubed

8 ounces cream cheese, softened

8 ounces canned crushed pineapple, drained

1 cup chopped pecans

Dissolve gelatin in water. Chill but do not congeal. With mixer, blend avocados with cream cheese. Mix in pineapple and pecans. Whip into gelatin. Pour into 8 inch square dish or greased 6 cup mold. Cover and refrigerate until set. *Must be prepared ahead.*

Serves 12

Sunshine Apricot Salad

Surprising accompaniment

6 ounces apricot gelatin
2 cups boiling water
3 ounces cream cheese, softened
8 ounces canned crushed pineapple, drained
2 large carrots, shredded
8 ounces frozen whipped topping, thawed
½ cup chopped pecans

Dissolve gelatin in water and refrigerate until partially congealed. With mixer, blend cream cheese and pineapple. Stir in carrots and gelatin. Refrigerate until partially congealed. Fold in whipped topping and pecans. Pour into greased 8 cup mold and refrigerate until set. *Must be prepared ahead.*

Serves 10

Pretzel Fruit Salad

League favorite

2 cups crushed pretzels
¼ cup sugar
¾ cup butter, melted
8 ounces cream cheese, softened
1 cup sugar
1½ cups frozen whipped topping, thawed
2 cups pineapple juice
6 ounces strawberry gelatin
20 ounces frozen strawberries

Mix pretzels, ¼ cup sugar and butter. Press into 13x9 inch baking dish. Bake at 350° for 10 minutes. Cool. With mixer, blend cream cheese and 1 cup sugar. Fold in whipped topping. Spread over crumb mixture and set aside. In saucepan, heat pineapple juice, add gelatin and stir until dissolved. Pour into large bowl, mix in strawberries and refrigerate until partially congealed. Spread over cream cheese mixture and refrigerate until set. *Must be prepared ahead.*

Serves 12

Triple Molded Salad
Elaborate appearance

First Layer

3 ounces lime gelatin

1 cup boiling water

9 ounces canned sliced pineapple, drained, reserving juice

2 tablespoons lemon juice

In bowl, dissolve gelatin in water and cool to room temperature. In measuring cup, combine pineapple juice, lemon juice and enough water to equal 1 cup. Stir into gelatin and refrigerate until partially congealed. Cut pineapple slices into thirds and arrange in an 'S' design in bottom of 9x5 inch loaf pan or greased 8 cup mold. Using part of gelatin mixture, just cover pineapple and refrigerate until set. Pour on remaining gelatin mixture and refrigerate until set.

Second Layer

3 ounces lemon gelatin

1 cup boiling water

6 ounces cream cheese, softened

⅓ cup mayonnaise

Dissolve gelatin in water and refrigerate until partially congealed. With mixer, blend cream cheese and mayonnaise and set aside. Whip gelatin until light and fluffy and fold into cream cheese mixture. Pour over lime gelatin layer and refrigerate until set.

Third Layer

3 ounces raspberry gelatin

2 cups boiling water

2 bananas, sliced

Dissolve gelatin in water. Cool to room temperature. Arrange banana slices on lemon layer. Using part of raspberry gelatin, just cover bananas. Refrigerate until set. Pour on remaining gelatin and refrigerate until set. *Must be prepared ahead.*

Serves 12

Fresh Fruit Salad Dressing
A change of pace

¼ cup sugar
½ teaspoon salt
1½ tablespoons flour
1 egg
2 tablespoons cider vinegar
¾ cup pineapple juice

Place sugar in small saucepan. Whisking after each addition, add salt, flour, egg, vinegar and pineapple juice. Cook over low heat, whisking continuously, until thickened and smooth. Chill. *Must be prepared ahead.*

Serves 8

French Salad Dressing
For fruit or green salad

1¾ cups sugar
¼ cup catsup
¾ cup vinegar
1 teaspoon salt
1 teaspoon paprika
1 cup salad oil

In quart container, mix sugar, catsup, vinegar, salt and paprika. Add oil, mixing well. *May be prepared ahead. Will keep indefinitely unrefrigerated.*

Serves 12

Water Chestnut Salad Dressing
Served over spinach in a California tea room

2 tablespoons sugar
½ teaspoon salt
½ teaspoon dry mustard
½ tablespoon onion juice
2 teaspoons lemon juice
3 tablespoons cider vinegar
½ cup salad oil
½ cup sliced water chestnuts, drained

Mix sugar, salt, mustard, onion juice, lemon juice, vinegar and oil. Add water chestnuts and marinate for at least 1 hour. *Must be prepared ahead.*

Serves 8

Vinaigrette Dressing

French classic

¼ teaspoon salt
Coarsely ground pepper to taste
1 teaspoon Dijon mustard
1 shallot, minced
3 tablespoons wine vinegar
½ cup olive oil
½ tablespoon lemon juice

In small mixing bowl, whisk salt, pepper, mustard, shallot and vinegar. Slowly add olive oil, whisking continuously. Stir in lemon juice. *May be prepared ahead.*

Serves 8

Caesar Salad Dressing

Quickly mixed. . .gourmet quality

1½ tablespoons lime juice
1 egg
1 garlic clove, minced
⅛ teaspoon Worcestershire sauce
⅓ cup grated Parmesan cheese
⅓ cup salad oil

Combine all ingredients in ½ pint container. Cover and shake well. Chill. *Must be prepared ahead.*

Serves 8

Spinach Salad Dressing

Tangy, exciting flavor

1/2 cup salad oil
3 tablespoons white wine vinegar
1 tablespoon minced onion
2 teaspoons Dijon mustard
1 teaspoon salt
1 teaspoon sugar
Coarsely ground pepper to taste

Combine all ingredients in 1/2 pint container. Cover and shake well. Chill. *Must be prepared ahead.*

Serves 8

Sesame Seed Dressing

Dress up your everyday salads

1/2 cup sesame seed
1 cup sugar
1 teaspoon paprika
1/2 teaspoon dry mustard
1 cup cider vinegar
1 teaspoon salt
1 teaspoon Worcestershire sauce
1 tablespoon minced onion
2 cups salad oil

Toast sesame seed in 200° oven until lightly brown. In 1 quart container, add all ingredients, cover and shake well. Chill. *Must be prepared ahead.*

Serves 20

Winning the meat and potatoes game every time

Steak Diane
Choice selection

4 filet mignon or boneless sirloin steaks
2 tablespoons olive oil
2 tablespoons butter
3 tablespoons chopped chives
2 tablespoons cognac
3 tablespoons snipped parsley
1 teaspoon dry mustard
½ teaspoon Worcestershire sauce
2 teaspoons beef broth
1 tablespoon butter
Pepper to taste

Pound steaks to ¼ inch thickness. Heat oil and 2 tablespoons butter in large frying pan until hot. Add steaks and cook 1½ minutes on 1 side, turn and cook 30 seconds. Transfer to warm serving dish. Into frying pan, stir chives and cook for 10 seconds. Add cognac, stirring well. Mix in parsley, mustard, Worcestershire sauce and beef broth. Stir in remaining 1 tablespoon butter. Sprinkle with pepper and pour over steaks.

Serves 4

Beef Tenderloin with Mushroom Sauce
Grand company entree

½ teaspoon coarsely ground pepper
1 (4 pound) beef tenderloin
2 teaspoons minced onion
½ pound fresh mushrooms, sliced
2 tablespoons butter
¾ ounce brown gravy mix, prepared
⅛ teaspoon dry mustard
2 tablespoons dry red wine

Sprinkle pepper over meat and place, fat side up, in roasting pan. Broil at 425° for 40 minutes or until done. To prepare sauce, saute onion and mushrooms in butter until tender. Mix with brown gravy. Stir in mustard and wine. Simmer for 5 minutes, stirring occasionally. Serve over sliced beef.

Serves 8

Brisket in a Bag

Unusual method with superb results

2 bay leaves

1 large onion, chopped

2 garlic cloves, pressed

1 cup barbecue sauce

1 cup salad oil

½ cup vinegar

1 celery rib, chopped

1 tablespoon prepared mustard

1 tablespoon pepper

¼ cup Liquid Smoke

1 (8 to 10 pound) vacuum packed untrimmed brisket

Additional barbecue sauce

Buns (optional)

Mix bay leaves, onion, garlic, 1 cup barbecue sauce, oil, vinegar, celery, mustard, pepper and Liquid Smoke. Pour over brisket in vacuum packed or large oven cooking bag and marinate for 1 to 3 days in refrigerator. Bake at 175° for 27 hours. Slice and trim meat. Serve with barbecue sauce. May be served on buns. *Must be prepared ahead.*

Serves 10

Barbecue Sauce

1 cup catsup

½ cup cider vinegar

1 teaspoon sugar

1 teaspoon chili powder

¼ teaspoon salt

1½ cups water

1 garlic clove, minced

2 tablespoons chopped onion

4 tablespoons butter

¼ cup Worcestershire sauce

1 teaspoon paprika

Pepper to taste

2 tablespoons flour (optional)

¼ cup water (optional)

In large saucepan, mix catsup, vinegar, sugar, chili powder, salt, 1½ cups water, garlic, onion, butter, Worcestershire sauce, paprika and pepper. Bring to a boil and simmer for 15 minutes. Remove from heat and strain. May be thickened by blending flour with ¼ cup water and stirring into sauce. *May be prepared ahead.*

Crockpot Brisket
Outdoor flavor

1 (5 pound) brisket
2 tablespoons Liquid Smoke
14 ounces catsup
½ cup red wine vinegar
½ cup soy sauce
1 tablespoon Worcestershire sauce
1 tablespoon steak sauce
Tabasco sauce to taste
½ cup corn syrup
1 teaspoon garlic powder
Dry mustard to taste
6 ounces lemon lime soft drink

Place brisket in crockpot. Combine Liquid Smoke, catsup, vinegar, soy sauce, Worcestershire sauce, steak sauce, Tabasco sauce, corn syrup, garlic powder, mustard and soft drink, mixing well. Pour over brisket. Cook on high heat for 1½ hours or until sauce is bubbly. Reduce heat to low and cook for 6½ hours or until done.

Serves 6

Southwestern Stew
Full flavored

1½ pounds round steak, cubed
2 to 3 pounds pork roast, cubed
2 onions, chopped
56 ounces canned taco sauce
1 teaspoon garlic salt
⅛ teaspoon garlic powder
½ teaspoon chili powder
24 ounces canned chopped green chilies
½ teaspoon sugar
½ teaspoon salt
½ teaspoon pepper
¼ teaspoon cayenne pepper

Mix all ingredients in stockpot. Simmer for 6 hours or until done. *May be prepared ahead. May be frozen.*

Serves 12

Deluxe Mulligan Stew

An uptown version

1½ pounds beef stew meat

2 tablespoons butter

1 garlic clove, minced

1 green pepper, chopped

1½ cups water

1 cup Burgundy

½ teaspoon sugar

2 teaspoons salt

½ teaspoon allspice

¼ teaspoon pepper

⅛ teaspoon basil

⅛ teaspoon oregano

6 small carrots, sliced

2 potatoes, peeled and chopped

1 small onion, chopped

17 ounces canned small green
   peas, drained

2 tablespoons flour (optional)

¼ cup water (optional)

Biscuits (optional)

In stockpot, brown meat in butter with garlic. Reduce heat to medium low and mix in green pepper, 1½ cups water, Burgundy, sugar, salt, allspice, pepper, basil and oregano. Cover and simmer for 1 hour or until meat is tender. Add additional water if necessary. Mix in carrots, potatoes and onion, cooking until vegetables are tender. Gently stir in peas and heat thoroughly. May be thickened by blending flour with water and stirring into stew. May be served over biscuits. *May be prepared ahead. May be frozen.*

Serves 6

Mexican Hash

Spicy entree from leftovers

3 cups cubed cooked roast beef or steak

3 tablespoons oil for frying

1 large onion, coarsely chopped

1 tomato, coarsely chopped

1 large jalapeno pepper, chopped

2 tablespoons chili powder

1 tablespoon cumin

1 tablespoon caraway seed

10 ounces beef consomme

2½ cups water

2 potatoes, peeled and coarsely chopped

Flour tortillas (optional)

In stockpot, brown beef in hot oil, stirring for 2 to 3 minutes. Mix in onion, tomato, jalapeno pepper, chili powder, cumin, caraway seed, beef consomme and water. Cook over low heat for 30 minutes. Mix in potatoes, cover and cook for 30 minutes or until potatoes are tender. Stir occasionally and add more water if necessary. May be wrapped in buttered flour tortillas. *May be prepared ahead. May be frozen.*

Serves 6

Swedish Meat Loaf

From the old country

1½ pounds ground beef

1 egg, well beaten

½ cup cracker or dry bread crumbs

½ teaspoon seasoned salt

½ teaspoon onion salt

¼ teaspoon pepper

2 tablespoons minced onion

¼ cup catsup

¼ cup milk

10 ounces tomato soup

¾ cup water

Mix beef, egg, crumbs, seasoned salt, onion salt, pepper, onion, catsup and milk. Shape into greased 8x4 inch loaf pan and bake at 400° for 10 minutes. Blend soup and water. Pour half around meat. Reduce heat to 350° and bake for 35 minutes. Pour remaining soup mixture over meat and bake for 10 minutes. *May be prepared ahead. May be frozen.*

Serves 6

Chili

Winter winner

3 pounds ground chuck	
2 tablespoons oil for frying	
1 small onion, chopped	
3 garlic cloves, minced	
¼ teaspoon pepper	
½ teaspoon garlic salt	
28 ounces canned whole tomatoes, chopped	
16 ounces tomato sauce	
4½ tablespoons chili powder	
2 tablespoons cumin	
1 tablespoon sugar	
4 cups water	
Canned Ranch Style beans (optional)	
Chopped jalapeno pepper (optional)	
¼ cup masa harina	
1 cup water	

In large stockpot, brown chuck in oil with onion, garlic, pepper and garlic salt. Mix in tomatoes, tomato sauce, chili powder, cumin, sugar and 4 cups water. Mix in beans and jalapeno pepper if desired. Simmer briskly for 2 hours, stirring frequently. Add additional water if necessary. Combine masa harina with 1 cup water and stir until thickened. Stir into chili at serving time. *May be prepared ahead. May be frozen.*

Serves 10

Individual Meat Pies

Family treat

2 (1 pound) loaves frozen bread dough
1½ pounds ground beef
1 garlic clove, minced
1 onion, coarsely chopped
Salt to taste
Pepper to taste
Flour for dusting
2 cups grated Cheddar cheese
Jalapeno pepper slices

Partially thaw dough. Slice each loaf into 9 pieces. Place on greased baking sheet for 1½ hours or until completely thawed and rising. In frying pan, saute beef, garlic and onion. Drain and season with salt and pepper. Cool. Dust each piece of dough with flour and gently shape into 4 to 5 inch circle. Place 2 tablespoons meat mixture, cheese and jalapeno peppers on dough. Fold in ½ and pinch edges to seal. Place on greased baking sheet and bake at 350° for 20 minutes or until lightly browned. *May be prepared ahead. May be frozen.*

Serves 6

Italian Beef Dip

Versatile entree that men favor

1 (3 to 3½ pound) boneless beef rump roast
2 cups hot water
2 beef bouillon cubes
1 teaspoon salt
½ teaspoon pepper
1 teaspoon oregano
⅛ teaspoon garlic salt
2 green peppers, sliced
4 tablespoons butter
Italian bread

In roasting pan, cook meat at 450° for 30 minutes. Combine water, bouillon cubes, salt, pepper, oregano and garlic salt, mixing well. Pour over meat. Reduce heat to 350° and cook for 2½ hours or until tender. Reserving liquid, remove meat, cool and thinly slice. In frying pan, saute green pepper in butter until lightly brown. Cover and steam for 20 minutes. Serve green pepper and meat on Italian bread and use reserved liquid for dipping. *May be prepared ahead, keeping meat and green pepper warm in roasting pan with liquid.*

Serves 6

Saturday Night Special

Double for now . . . Save half for later

1 pound ground beef
1 small onion, chopped
1 green pepper, chopped
½ pound fresh mushrooms, sliced
14 ounces canned whole kernel corn, drained
1 cup grated Cheddar cheese
10 ounces tomato soup
14 ounces canned whole tomatoes
¾ teaspoon salt
½ teaspoon chili powder
½ teaspoon Worcestershire sauce
7 ounces ready cut spaghetti, cooked and drained

In frying pan, brown meat, onion, green pepper and mushrooms. Set aside. In large bowl, mix corn, cheese, soup, tomatoes, salt, chili powder, Worcestershire sauce and spaghetti. Stir in meat mixture. Transfer to greased 1½ quart baking dish. Bake at 325° for 45 minutes. *May be prepared ahead. May be frozen.*

Serves 6

California Casserole

Mexican lasagne

2 pounds ground round or chuck
1 large onion, chopped
1 garlic clove, minced
2 tablespoons chili powder
24 ounces tomato sauce
½ teaspoon sugar
½ tablespoon salt
4 ounces canned chopped green chilies
½ cup sliced ripe olives
12 corn tortillas
Oil for frying
1 egg
2 cups small curd cottage cheese
8 ounces Monterey Jack cheese, thinly sliced
1 cup grated Cheddar cheese
Chopped green onion
Sour cream
Sliced ripe olives

In stockpot, brown meat with onion and garlic. Pour off grease. Sprinkle meat with chili powder, mixing well. Stir in tomato sauce, sugar, salt, green chilies and ½ cup olives. Simmer for 15 minutes. In frying pan, cook but do not brown tortillas in hot oil. Drain and quarter. Beat egg with cottage cheese and set aside. In greased 11x7 inch baking dish, spread ⅓ of meat mixture. Cover with ½ of Monterey Jack cheese, ½ of cottage cheese mixture and ½ of tortillas. Repeat, ending with meat layer. Top with Cheddar cheese. Bake at 350° for 3C minutes or until thoroughly heated. Garnish with green onion, sour cream and olives. *May be prepared ahead and refrigerated or frozen before baking.*

Serves 6

Beef Tortini

One dish meal with Italian flavor

2 pounds ground beef

1 onion, chopped

16 ounces tomato sauce

16 ounces tomato paste

20 ounces frozen chopped spinach, cooked and drained

3 cups cottage cheese

¼ cup sugar

2 cups grated mozzarella cheese

6 ounces canned sliced mushrooms, drained

12 ounces egg noodles, cooked and drained

In frying pan, brown beef and onion. Pour off grease. Add tomato sauce and tomato paste. Simmer for 20 minutes, stirring occasionally. In mixing bowl, mix spinach, cottage cheese and sugar. In greased 13x9 inch baking dish, layer meat mixture then spinach mixture. Repeat. Top with mozzarella cheese and mushrooms. Bake at 325° for 30 minutes. Serve over noodles. *May be prepared ahead. May be frozen before or after baking.*

Serves 8

Easy Beef Stroganoff

Makes an everyday meal special

1 pound round steak, cut into ½ inch strips

4 tablespoons butter

½ pound fresh mushrooms, sliced

1 onion, chopped

1 cup beef broth

1 cup sour cream

2½ tablespoons flour

Cooked rice or noodles

In frying pan, quickly brown meat in butter. Move meat to 1 side of pan and add mushrooms and onion. Stir and cook until tender. Add beef broth to meat and vegetables, mixing well. Simmer for 1 hour. Blend sour cream and flour. Add to mixture and cook, stirring until thickened. Serve over rice or noodles. *Meat mixture may be prepared ahead.*

Serves 4

Chilighetti
Spicy and excites hunger

1 pound ground chuck
1 garlic clove, minced
1 large onion, chopped
28 ounces canned whole tomatoes, chopped
38 ounces canned chili
3 cups grated Cheddar cheese
7 ounces spaghetti, cooked and drained
1 cup sour cream
Freshly grated Parmesan cheese

In Dutch oven, brown chuck with garlic and onion. Pour off grease. Stir in tomatoes and chili and simmer for 45 minutes, stirring occasionally. In large bowl, mix Cheddar cheese and spaghetti. Fold in sour cream. Mix with meat in Dutch oven and top with Parmesan cheese. Cover and bake at 350° for 45 minutes. *May be prepared ahead. May be frozen.*

Serves 8

Rock Cornish Hens
Parmesan
Gourmet quality with ease

2 Rock Cornish game hens
1 teaspoon vegetable salt
1 shallot, minced
2 teaspoons butter
¼ cup finely snipped parsley
2 tablespoons grated Parmesan cheese
Cooked wild rice (optional)

Rub hens, inside and out, with vegetable salt and set aside. In small frying pan, saute shallots in butter for 1 minute. Stir in parsley and Parmesan cheese. Cool and stuff between skin and flesh of hens. Bake in shallow baking dish at 425° for 40 minutes or until done. Cut in ½. May be served over wild rice. *May be prepared ahead before cooking.*

Serves 4

Tarragon Roasted Cornish Hens

A touch of cream, hmmm

3 Rock Cornish game hens
2 teaspoons salt
½ teaspoon white pepper
2 teaspoons tarragon
½ cup butter, melted
1 cup chicken broth
1 cup dry sauterne
1 cup half and half

Rub hens, inside and out, with salt and pepper. Sprinkle each cavity with tarragon. Tie legs together and brush hens with butter. Place in Dutch oven and bake at 400° for 1 hour, basting frequently with chicken broth mixed with sauterne. Remove hens, reserving liquid, and cool to handling. Remove backbone and disjoint. Set aside. Place Dutch oven on stovetop and heat liquid until reduced by ½. Stir in half and half and bring to a boil. Strain and serve as a sauce over hens. *May be prepared ahead.*

Serves 6

Chicken Tarragon

All time classic

2 teaspoons seasoned salt
¼ teaspoon pepper
1/8 teaspoon paprika
1 fryer, cut up
4 tablespoons butter
1 onion, thinly sliced
3 ounces canned sliced mushrooms, drained
2 teaspoons tarragon
¼ cup water

Mix seasoned salt, pepper and paprika. Sprinkle over chicken. In frying pan, brown chicken slowly in butter then remove from pan. Add onion to pan and cook until tender. Move onion to 1 side and return chicken to pan. Top chicken with mushrooms and onion. Sprinkle with tarragon, add water, cover and simmer for 40 minutes or until chicken is tender.

Serves 4

Chicken Crabmeat Supreme
Editor's choice

8 boneless chicken breast halves

3 tablespoons butter

¼ cup flour

¾ cup milk

¾ cup chicken broth

⅓ cup dry white wine

1 small onion, chopped

1 tablespoon butter

6 ounces fresh or frozen crabmeat

3 ounces canned chopped mushrooms, drained

½ cup cracker crumbs

2 tablespoons snipped parsley

¼ teaspoon salt

Pepper to taste

1 cup grated Swiss cheese

Paprika

Parsley

Pound chicken into 8x5 inch pieces. Set aside. In saucepan, melt 3 tablespoons butter and blend in flour. Add milk, chicken broth and wine. Stir and heat until mixture is thickened and bubbly. Set aside. In frying pan, saute onion in 1 tablespoon butter until tender. Stir in crabmeat, mushrooms, cracker crumbs, parsley, salt and pepper. Add 2 tablespoons sauce and stir. Spoon onto chicken, fold in sides and roll. Place seam side down in 13x9 inch baking dish and pour on remaining sauce. Cover and bake at 350° for 1 hour. Uncover, sprinkle with cheese and paprika. Bake until cheese melts. Garnish with parsley. *May be prepared ahead.*

Serves 8

Chicken Cordon Bleu

Try our version

6 boneless whole chicken breasts

6 thin provolone cheese slices

6 prosciutto ham slices

Flour

Salt to taste

White pepper to taste

2 eggs, lightly beaten

1½ cups dry bread crumbs

Butter

Olive oil

Pound chicken breasts until flat. Top with cheese and ham. Fold and seal by lightly pounding edges. Set aside. In dish, mix flour, salt and pepper. In separate dishes, place eggs and crumbs. Dredge chicken in flour, brush with egg and roll in crumbs. Shake off excess crumbs. In frying pan, heat equal amounts of butter and olive oil over medium heat. Add chicken, cook on all sides until golden brown and drain. Serve with sauce. *May be prepared ahead and refrigerated on cake rack until ready to cook. May be frozen.*

Serves 6

Sauce

1 shallot, chopped

2 tablespoons butter

8 to 10 fresh mushrooms, sliced

3 tablespoons flour

1½ cups chicken broth

¼ cup white wine

½ cup half and half

Salt to taste

Pepper to taste

½ teaspoon snipped parsley

Saute shallot in butter. Stir in mushrooms and cook until tender. Blend in flour then stir in chicken broth and wine. Simmer for 20 minutes. Add half and half and bring to a boil. Season with salt and pepper. Mix in parsley.

Poulet Dijonnaise in Phyllo

A prize winner

4 tablespoons unsalted butter
3 boneless whole chicken breasts, cut into 1 inch strips
Salt to taste
White pepper to taste
1/2 cup Dijon mustard
2 cups whipping cream
1/2 cup white wine
5 phyllo pastry sheets
1/4 cup butter, melted
1/4 cup dry bread crumbs
1 egg
1 teaspoon water

Melt 4 tablespoons butter in large frying pan over medium heat. Sprinkle chicken with salt and pepper. Add to pan and cook for 5 minutes or until no longer pink. Do not overcook. Remove to platter, reserving drippings, and keep warm. Whisk in mustard with drippings. Add whipping cream and wine and whisk until well blended. Reduce heat to low and simmer until sauce is slightly thickened and reduced by 1/4. Stir in any liquid from platter and cook until slightly reduced. Strain sauce over chicken and toss until completely coated. Place 1 sheet of pastry on dry dish towel, brush with part of butter and sprinkle with 1 tablespoon bread crumbs. Repeat pastry, butter and bread crumbs 3 times. Top with last sheet of pastry and brush borders with melted butter. Leaving 2 inch border on all sides, arrange chicken over bottom 1/3 of long side of pastry. Turn up bottom edge, partially enclosing chicken, and fold in sides. Roll jelly roll style and place, seam side down, on baking sheet. In small bowl, beat egg with water and brush on dough. Bake at 450° for 12 minutes or until pastry is crisp and golden brown. To serve, cut into 1/2 inch slices. *May be prepared ahead, covered and refrigerated before glazing and baking.*

Serves 6

Sherried Chicken

Sour cream and sherry. . .a delightful blend

1 pound fresh mushrooms, sliced

Chopped chives to taste

2 tablespoons butter

8 boneless chicken breast halves

Salt to taste

Garlic salt to taste

Pepper to taste

10 ounces cream of mushroom soup

10 ounces cream of chicken soup

Ripe olive halves to taste

1/4 cup sherry

2 cups sour cream

Sherry (optional)

In frying pan, saute mushrooms and chives in butter. Sprinkle chicken with salt, garlic salt and pepper. Add to pan and brown lightly. Add soups and olives, stirring well. Mix in sherry, cover and simmer for 45 minutes. Blend in sour cream and additional sherry if desired. *May be prepared ahead.*

Serves 4

Parmesan Chicken Dijon

Plain chicken made fancy

2 cups dry bread crumbs

1 1/4 cups grated Parmesan cheese

1/3 cup snipped parsley

1 1/2 cups butter

1 garlic clove, pressed

1 tablespoon Dijon mustard

1/2 tablespoon Worcestershire sauce

4 whole chicken breasts

In shallow dish, mix bread crumbs, Parmesan cheese and parsley. Set aside. Melt butter in saucepan and mix with garlic, mustard and Worcestershire sauce. Cool slightly. Dip chicken in butter mixture and roll in crumbs. Arrange in 13x9 inch baking dish and cook at 350° for 1 hour, basting occasionally with remaining butter mixture. *May be prepared ahead.*

Serves 4

Poppy Seed Chicken

Ritzy way with chicken

4 pounds chicken breast, cooked, boned and chopped

20 ounces cream of chicken soup

2 cups sour cream

1/2 cup white wine

2 1/2 cups Ritz cracker crumbs

1/2 cup butter, melted

Poppy seed

Arrange chicken in greased 13x9 inch baking dish. Set aside. Blend soup, sour cream and wine. Pour over chicken. Sprinkle with mixture of cracker crumbs and butter. Cover with poppy seed. Bake at 350° for 35 minutes. *May be prepared ahead.*

Serves 8

Chicken Rockefeller

New way for an old standard

1 cup seasoned bread crumbs

3 tablespoons grated Parmesan cheese

12 boneless chicken breast halves

Salt to taste

Pepper to taste

10 ounces frozen chopped spinach, cooked, drained and cooled

1 egg, beaten

1 tablespoon grated Parmesan cheese

3 tablespoons butter, melted

In shallow pan, mix bread crumbs and 3 tablespoons Parmesan cheese. Set aside. Sprinkle chicken with salt and pepper and dredge in crumb mixture. Reserve remaining crumb mixture. Arrange chicken in 13x9 inch baking dish and set aside. Mix spinach with egg and 1 tablespoon Parmesan cheese. Mound on chicken, sprinkle with reserved crumb mixture and drizzle with butter. Bake at 350° for 40 minutes. *May be prepared ahead. May be frozen.*

Serves 6

Swiss Chicken

Delicate, cheesy and creamy

3 tablespoons flour

½ tablespoon paprika

1 teaspoon salt

6 boneless whole chicken breasts

2 tablespoons butter

1 tablespoon oil for frying

¼ cup dry sherry

1 teaspoon cornstarch

¾ cup half and half

⅓ cup dry white wine

1 tablespoon lemon juice

6 baby Swiss cheese slices

In bag, mix flour, paprika and salt. Add chicken, 1 piece at a time, shaking until well coated. In large frying pan over medium high heat, brown chicken in butter and oil. Stir in sherry, cover and simmer for 25 minutes or until tender. Remove chicken, reserving drippings, and keep warm. Mix cornstarch and half and half and stir into drippings. Cook and stir until sauce is thickened. Stir in wine and lemon juice, heating for 2 to 3 minutes. Return chicken to pan and top with cheese. Cover, remove from heat and let stand for 5 minutes.

Serves 6

Chicken Alberghetti

Italian food lovers' favorite

4 tablespoons butter

¼ cup oil for frying

4 boneless chicken breast halves

2 eggs, beaten

Seasoned bread crumbs

8 to 10 fresh mushrooms, sliced

1 cup tomato sauce

½ cup half and half

4 mozzarella cheese slices

4 Swiss cheese slices

½ cup freshly grated Parmesan cheese

In frying pan, heat butter and oil. Dip chicken in eggs and roll in bread crumbs. Saute until golden brown. Remove chicken and set aside. Add mushrooms to pan and saute. For sauce, mix tomato sauce with half and half. Cover bottom of 8 inch square baking dish with ½ of sauce. Arrange chicken over sauce and top with mushrooms. Place mozzarella and Swiss cheeses over chicken, cover with remaining sauce and sprinkle with Parmesan cheese. Bake at 325° for 45 minutes or until done. *May be prepared ahead.*

Serves 4

Chicken Scallopini

Excellent Italian recipe

2 pounds boneless chicken breast, cut into ¼ inch slices
Salt to taste
Pepper to taste
2 tablespoons olive oil
4 tablespoons butter
2 onions, chopped
1 garlic clove, chopped
¼ cup Madeira
1 tablespoon lemon juice
½ cup whipping cream
6 lemon slices
6 tablespoons chopped almonds
2 tablespoons butter

Sprinkle chicken with salt and pepper. Set aside. In frying pan, heat olive oil and 4 tablespoons butter, add onion and garlic and saute until tender. Remove from pan and set aside. Add chicken and saute until golden brown. Return onion and garlic to pan, stirring once. Add Madeira, cooking and stirring until liquid is reduced by ½. Add lemon juice, stirring once. Add cream, cooking and stirring until sauce is heated thoroughly. Place in serving dish and top with lemon slices and almonds that have been browned in 2 tablespoons butter.

Serves 4

Easy Gourmet Chicken

Special enough to serve guests

½ pound fresh mushrooms, sliced
4 boneless chicken breast halves
Seasoned salt to taste
Pepper to taste
Curry powder to taste
4 tablespoons butter
¾ cup sherry
1 cup whipping cream
Cooked brown or wild rice

Arrange mushrooms in greased 8 inch square baking dish. Sprinkle chicken with seasoned salt and pepper. Rub curry powder in cavity of each breast. Place chicken, cavity side down, over mushrooms and dot with butter. Pour sherry over chicken and bake at 350° for 1 hour. Top with cream and bake for 20 minutes. Serve over brown or wild rice. *May be prepared ahead and refrigerated before adding sherry.*

Serves 4

Creamed Chicken and Shrimp

Simple but great for company

8 boneless chicken breast halves

½ pound fresh mushrooms, sliced

2 garlic cloves, minced

4 tablespoons butter

20 ounces cream of mushroom soup

½ cup half and half

¼ cup grated Parmesan cheese

1 pound cooked and peeled shrimp

4 cups cooked rice

½ cup butter, melted

¼ cup sliced water chestnuts

In frying pan, brown chicken, mushrooms and garlic in 4 tablespoons butter. Stir in soup, half and half and Parmesan cheese. Cover and cook over low heat for 45 minutes. Add shrimp and cook for 15 minutes or until chicken is done and shrimp is heated. Just before serving, mix rice with melted butter and water chestnuts. Serve chicken and shrimp over rice mixture.

Serves 8

Chinese Chicken

Your wok makes this one easy

¼ cup oil for frying
4 boneless whole chicken breasts, cubed
1 celery rib, coarsely chopped
2 tablespoons soy sauce
1 teaspoon salt
¼ teaspoon pepper
6 ounces canned sliced mushrooms, drained, reserving liquid
6 ounces canned bean sprouts, drained, reserving liquid
1 tablespoon cornstarch
Cooked rice or chow mein noodles
Toasted almonds

In hot oil, stir fry chicken for 10 minutes. Stir in celery and soy sauce and cook for 5 minutes. Sprinkle with salt and pepper. Add mushrooms and bean sprouts, stirring well. In small bowl, mix reserved liquids from mushrooms and bean sprouts with cornstarch. Add to pan and cook, stirring continuously, until thickened and clear. Serve over rice or chow mein noodles. Sprinkle with almonds.

Serves 4

Sweet and Sour Chicken

Chinese cuisine simplified

1 fryer, cut up
8 ounces French dressing
8 ounces apricot preserves
⅓ cup dry onion soup mix
Cooked rice (optional)

Arrange chicken in 2 quart shallow casserole. Top with mixture of dressing, preserves and soup mix. Cover and bake at 350° for 1 hour and 15 minutes. Uncover and bake 15 minutes. May be served over rice. *May be prepared ahead.*

Serves 4

Mom's Stewed Chicken

A roux is the base of this family favorite

1 cup flour

½ teaspoon cayenne pepper

½ teaspoon garlic salt

½ teaspoon Nature's Seasoning

2 fryers, cut up

½ cup oil for frying

2 tablespoons salad oil

2 tablespoons flour

1 large onion, chopped

½ cup chopped green pepper

1 celery rib, chopped

1 garlic clove, minced

28 ounces canned whole tomatoes

16 ounces tomato sauce

1 cup water

½ teaspoon oregano

¼ teaspoon garlic powder

Salt to taste

Pepper to taste

12 ounces spaghetti, cooked and drained

In bag, mix 1 cup flour, cayenne pepper, garlic salt and Nature's Seasoning. Add chicken, 1 piece at a time, shaking until well coated. In stockpot, heat ½ cup oil and brown chicken. Remove chicken, reserving drippings, and set aside. Whisk in 2 tablespoons oil and 2 tablespoons flour with drippings. Stir and heat until thickened and brown. Add onion, green pepper, celery and garlic. Saute, stirring occasionally, until tender. Stir in tomatoes, tomato sauce and water. Simmer for 5 minutes. Stir in oregano, garlic powder, salt and pepper. Add chicken and simmer for 1 hour or until chicken is done. Serve over spaghetti. *Chicken may be prepared ahead and may be frozen.*

Serves 8

Chicken Florentine Casserole

Make two and freeze one

4 tablespoons butter

¼ cup flour

1 cup milk

1 cup chicken broth

5 ounces small egg noodles, cooked and drained

2 cups sour cream

⅓ cup lemon juice

10 ounces frozen chopped spinach, cooked and drained

8 ounces canned chopped mushrooms, drained

8 ounces sliced water chestnuts, drained

2 ounces diced pimiento

1 large onion, chopped

1 celery rib, chopped

2 teaspoons seasoned salt

1 teaspoon Accent

½ teaspoon cayenne pepper

1 teaspoon paprika

1 teaspoon salt

2 teaspoons pepper

2 fryers, cooked, boned and chopped

1½ cups grated Cheddar cheese

In stockpot, melt butter and blend with flour. Add milk and chicken broth. Cook over low heat, stirring continuously, until thickened. Mix in noodles, sour cream, lemon juice, spinach, mushrooms, water chestnuts, pimiento, onion, celery, seasoned salt, Accent, cayenne pepper, paprika, salt and pepper. In greased 4 quart baking dish, alternate layers of noodle mixture and chicken. Top with cheese and bake at 350° for 30 minutes or until bubbly. *May be prepared ahead. May be frozen.*

Serves 12

Chicken Superb

A casserole for special occasions

6 tablespoons butter

6 tablespoons flour

½ tablespoon salt

½ teaspoon celery salt

Beau Monde seasoning to taste

2 cups chicken broth, heated

2 cups whipping cream, scalded

2 tablespoons sherry

Slivered almonds

¾ pound fresh mushrooms, sliced

6 ounces egg noodles, cooked and drained

Snipped parsley to taste

1 fryer, cooked, boned and chopped

Grated Cheddar cheese

In stockpot, melt butter, blend with flour and cook, but do not brown. Whisk in salt, celery salt, Beau Monde seasoning and chicken broth. Stir until thickened. Mix in cream, sherry, almonds, mushrooms, noodles, parsley and chicken. Pour into greased 13x9 inch baking dish. Top with cheese and bake at 350° for 40 minutes or until done. *May be prepared ahead. May be frozen.*

Serves 12

Chicken Spaghetti Olé

Family weekender

1 small onion, chopped
¼ cup chopped green pepper
3 tablespoons butter
1 fryer, cooked, boned and chopped
2 ounces diced pimiento
10 ounces canned tomatoes and green chilies, chopped
16 ounces Velveeta cheese, cubed
12 ounces spaghetti, cooked and drained

In frying pan, saute onion and green pepper in butter. Mix with chicken, pimiento, tomatoes and green chilies, cheese and spaghetti in large bowl. Bake in 13x9 inch baking dish at 350° until cheese is melted. *May be prepared ahead. May be frozen before baking.*

Serves 8

Chicken and Rice Bake

One dish entree for a busy day

10 ounces cream of mushroom soup
1¼ cups milk
⅓ cup dry onion soup mix
4 ounces canned chopped mushrooms, drained
1 cup uncooked rice
1 fryer, cut up

In 11x7 inch baking dish, mix mushroom soup, milk, onion soup mix, mushrooms and rice. Arrange chicken on top of mixture. Cover and bake at 350° for 1 hour. Uncover and bake for 15 minutes. *May be prepared ahead.*

Serves 4

Chicken and Wild Rice Casserole

Basic with a flair

4 pounds chicken pieces
2 quarts water
1 large onion, quartered
1 carrot
1 celery rib
3 tablespoons salt
3 tablespoons chopped onion
½ cup butter
¼ cup flour
6 ounces canned sliced mushrooms, drained, reserving liquid
1½ cups whipping cream
2 ounces diced pimiento
2 tablespoons snipped parsley
2 teaspoons salt
3 cups cooked wild rice
¼ cup slivered almonds

In Dutch oven, boil chicken in water with onion, carrot, celery and salt until done. Remove chicken, bone, chop and set aside. Strain and reserve broth. Discard vegetables. Saute 3 tablespoons onion in butter in Dutch oven. Blend in flour and remove from heat. In measuring cup, combine mushroom liquid with enough chicken broth for 1½ cups. Stir into flour mixture, return to heat and cook slowly. Add cream and stir continuously until thickened. Remove from heat and mix in mushrooms, pimiento, parsley, salt, chicken and rice. Sprinkle with almonds and bake at 350° for 30 minutes. *May be prepared ahead. May be frozen.*

Serves 8

Paella
A one pot feast

12 to 16 chicken pieces
Oil for frying
2 large onions, chopped
1 garlic clove
2 cups uncooked rice
16 ounces canned whole tomatoes, chopped
3 cups chicken broth
1 teaspoon basil or tarragon
1 small bay leaf
1 teaspoon paprika
¼ teaspoon turmeric
½ pound pepperoni, sliced
10 ounces frozen green peas, thawed
1 pound shrimp, cooked and peeled

In frying pan, brown chicken in oil. Remove, reserving drippings, and set aside. Saute onion and garlic in drippings until tender. Return chicken to pan and set aside. To prepare rice, substitute the amount of required water, according to package directions, with a combination of tomatoes and chicken broth. Place in Dutch oven and mix with basil or tarragon, bay leaf, paprika and turmeric. Heat to boiling, add rice, cover and simmer until liquid is reduced by ½. Mix in chicken and pepperoni. Cook until chicken and rice are done. If additional liquid is needed during cooking, mix remaining tomatoes with warm chicken broth and add to pot. Stir in peas and shrimp. Place in oven at 250° until thoroughly heated. *May be prepared ahead, adding peas and shrimp at cooking time.*

Serves 8

Company Chicken Casserole

A meal in one

1 large onion, chopped
2 celery ribs, chopped
30 ounces cream of celery soup
4 ounces diced pimiento
8 ounces canned sliced mushrooms, drained
1 cup mayonnaise
12 ounces uncooked long grain and wild rice
32 ounces canned French style green beans
4 pounds whole chicken breast, cooked, boned and chopped
1 cup slivered almonds
3 cups crushed potato chips

Blend onion, celery, soup, pimiento, mushrooms, mayonnaise, rice, green beans and chicken. Pour into 2 (13x9 inch) baking dishes. Cover and bake at 350° for 45 minutes. Sprinkle with almonds and bake uncovered for 45 minutes. Top with potato chips to serve. *May be prepared ahead.*

Serves 16

Chicken Tortilla Casserole

Tex Mex eating at its finest

4½ to 5 pounds chicken breast halves

24 corn tortillas

20 ounces cream of mushroom soup

20 ounces cream of chicken soup

30 ounces canned tomatoes and green chilies

2 large onions, chopped

2 large green peppers, chopped

½ cup butter

2 cups grated sharp Cheddar cheese

2 cups grated Monterey Jack cheese

In stockpot, boil chicken in water until done. Remove chicken, reserving broth, bone and cut into bite size pieces. Dip tortillas, 1 at a time, in broth and layer in 2 (13x9 inch) baking dishes. Top with layer of chicken and repeat. Set aside. Blend soups with tomatoes and green chilies and pour over chicken. Saute onion and green pepper in butter. Spoon onto casserole. With sharp knife, cut through casserole, making small squares. Sprinkle with cheeses and bake at 300° for 30 minutes or until bubbly. *May be prepared ahead. May be frozen.*

Serves 12

Dill Grilled Chicken

Surprise ingredient children will love

⅓ cup dill pickle juice

¾ cup mayonnaise

1 tablespoon chopped onion

½ teaspoon pepper

Garlic salt to taste

4 whole chicken breasts

Dill pickle slices

For sauce, mix pickle juice, mayonnaise, onion, pepper and garlic salt. Cook chicken on grill over medium heat for 20 minutes. Baste with sauce. Reduce heat to low and cook for 25 minutes or until chicken is done, turning and basting every 5 to 8 minutes. To serve, top with pickle slices and remaining sauce. *Sauce may be prepared ahead.*

Serves 4

Lemonade Chicken

For outdoor cooking

**12 ounces frozen pink
lemonade concentrate,
thawed**

⅔ cup soy sauce

2 teaspoons seasoned salt

¼ teaspoon garlic powder

8 boneless chicken breast halves

To prepare marinade, mix lemonade with soy sauce, seasoned salt and garlic powder. Pour over chicken, cover and refrigerate for several hours, turning occasionally. Cook chicken on grill for 15 minutes or until done. Turn and baste with marinade during cooking. *Must be prepared ahead.*

Serves 4

Herbed Roast Leg of Lamb

Will make lamb lovers out of everyone

1 (6 pound) leg of lamb

1 garlic clove

1 teaspoon salt

**1¼ teaspoons coarsely ground
pepper**

2 tablespoons olive oil

1 teaspoon marjoram

1 teaspoon rosemary

1 teaspoon thyme

1 tablespoon flour

1 cup dry white wine

1 cup water

Place lamb in shallow roasting pan. Press garlic in small bowl with salt and pepper then mix with olive oil. Rub mixture on lamb. Sprinkle with marjoram, rosemary, thyme and flour. Pour wine and water around lamb. Roast at 325° for 2½ to 3 hours, basting every 30 minutes. *May be prepared ahead and refrigerated before roasting.*

Serves 6

116

Ham Loaf with Mustard Sauce

Variation of meat loaf

1 pound ground ham
1 pound ground pork
1 cup Rice Krispies cereal, crushed
1 teaspoon salt
1 teaspoon pepper
2 eggs
1 cup milk

Combine all ingredients, mixing well, and shape into greased 8x4 inch loaf pan. Bake at 350° for 45 minutes. Brush loaf with ½ of sauce. Reduce heat to 250° and bake for 1½ hours. In saucepan, heat remaining sauce and serve with ham loaf. *May be prepared ahead.*

Serves 6

Sauce

½ cup brown sugar
¼ cup cider vinegar
½ cup water
1 teaspoon dry mustard

Mix all ingredients.

Ham and Asparagus Rolls

A delicious quickie

8 Swiss cheese slices
15 ounces canned asparagus spears, drained
8 (¼ inch) cooked ham slices
10 ounces Cheddar cheese soup
¼ cup sherry
Sliced toasted almonds

Place cheese and asparagus on ham. Roll and place, seam side down, in 11x7 inch baking dish. Blend soup with sherry and pour ½ over ham rolls. Sprinkle with almonds and bake at 350° for 15 minutes or until thoroughly heated. In saucepan, heat remaining sauce and serve with ham rolls.

Serves 4

Ham Empanadas
Spicy turnover

2 cups flour
½ teaspoon salt
1 cup butter
1 cup sour cream
½ cup ground ham
2 green onions, chopped
4 tablespoons canned chopped green chilies
¼ cup sour cream

To prepare dough, blend flour, salt, butter and 1 cup sour cream. Roll until thin and cut into 3 inch circles. To prepare filling, blend ham, onions, green chilies and ¼ cup sour cream. Place 1 tablespoon filling on dough. Fold and seal edges with fork. Bake at 375° for 15 minutes. Turn and bake for 10 minutes. *May be prepared ahead or frozen before baking.*

Serves 6

Ham and Apples
Classy way to serve leftover ham

3 cups coarsely chopped cooked ham
2 tablespoons prepared mustard
2 large apples, peeled, cored and sliced
Lemon juice
½ cup brown sugar
½ teaspoon grated orange peel
2 tablespoons flour

Arrange ham in 1½ quart baking dish and spread with mustard. Dip apple slices in lemon juice and arrange over ham. Mix brown sugar, orange peel and flour. Sprinkle over apples. Bake at 350° for 30 minutes or until done. *May be prepared ahead.*

Serves 4

Austrian Pork and Apples
Pork chops glorified

4 butterfly pork chops

3 unpeeled apples, cored and sliced

⅓ cup brown sugar

2 teaspoons cinnamon

3 tablespoons butter

Brown pork chops in frying pan. Layer apple slices in greased 11x7 inch baking dish. Sprinkle with brown sugar and cinnamon and dot with butter. Arrange pork chops over apples and cover. Bake at 350° for 1 hour or until done. *May be prepared ahead.*

Serves 4

Cheddar Cheese Pork Chops
Makes a wonderful gravy at the same time

½ cup water

4 boneless butterfly pork chops

Seasoned salt to taste

Pepper to taste

Garlic salt to taste

4 thick Cheddar cheese slices

1 large yellow or white onion, thickly sliced

20 ounces golden mushroom soup

Pour water into 11x7 inch baking dish. Sprinkle pork chops with seasoned salt, pepper and garlic salt. Arrange in baking dish. Top with cheese, onion and soup. Bake at 400° for 1 hour or until done. Use liquid in baking dish as sauce.

Serves 4

Italian Pork Chops
Serve your guests

2 tablespoons butter
2 teaspoons Italian salad dressing mix
4 (1 inch) pork chops
10 ounces cream of mushroom soup
½ tablespoon Italian salad dressing mix
4 ounces whipped cream cheese with chives
⅓ cup dry white wine

Melt butter in large frying pan and mix with 2 teaspoons salad dressing mix. Add pork chops and brown slowly on both sides. Transfer to 11x7 inch baking dish. In bowl, blend soup, ½ tablespoon salad dressing mix and cream cheese. Stir in wine and pour over meat. Cover and bake at 375° for 30 minutes. Uncover and bake for 15 minutes or until done. For variation, substitute chicken breasts for pork chops.

Serves 4

Deviled Pork Chops
Tangy and tasty

6 (1½ inch) pork chops
2 tablespoons butter, softened
½ cup chili sauce
½ cup catsup
2 tablespoons Worcestershire sauce
¼ cup prepared mustard
1 teaspoon salt
⅛ teaspoon cayenne pepper
½ cup water

Place pork chops in broiler pan. Blend butter, chili sauce, catsup, Worcestershire sauce, mustard, salt and cayenne pepper. Coat pork chops with part of sauce. Place under broiler to brown. Pour remaining sauce over chops, add water, cover and bake at 350° for 2 hours or until done. *May be prepared ahead.*

Serves 6

Barbecued Pork Sandwiches
Feed the group

1 pork roast
2 cups catsup
1 cup vinegar
3 tablespoons Worcestershire sauce
1 tablespoon prepared mustard
½ tablespoon Tabasco sauce
4 tablespoons butter
¼ to ½ cup brown sugar
Buns or hard rolls

In stockpot, boil meat in water for 4 hours or until meat is falling apart. Remove meat, cool and shred. Discard liquid. In same pot, add catsup, vinegar, Worcestershire sauce, mustard, Tabasco sauce, butter and brown sugar. Boil for 1 minute, stirring continuously. Mix in pork and simmer for 30 minutes. Serve on bread.

Serves 8

American Cassoulet
High protein casserole

8 ounces dried navy beans
2½ cups water
1 bay leaf
1 pound ground pork
1 large onion, chopped
1 green or red pepper, chopped
2 garlic cloves, minced
Salt to taste
Coarsely ground pepper to taste
½ pound smoked sausage, sliced
½ pound Italian sausage, sliced
6 small chicken pieces
2 tablespoons oil for frying
1 tablespoon tomato paste

In large saucepan, cover beans with water and soak overnight. To beans and water, add bay leaf and bring to a gentle boil. Simmer, stirring occasionally, for 2½ hours. Discard bay leaf and drain, reserving 1 cup liquid. Set aside. In large frying pan, brown pork with onion. Add green or red pepper, garlic, salt, pepper and smoked sausage. Remove casings from Italian sausage. Add sausage to frying pan and brown. Remove from heat and pour off grease. Set aside. In separate frying pan, brown chicken in oil and drain. In 2 quart baking dish, layer beans, then pork and repeat. Arrange chicken on top. Blend tomato paste with reserved bean liquid and pour over cassoulet. Bake at 350° for 1 hour. *Must be prepared ahead.*

Serves 6

Tangy Hotdogs
Ideal for soccer finale

6 tablespoons vinegar
3 tablespoons flour
3 onions, chopped
4½ tablespoons Worcestershire sauce
2 tablespoons salt
⅛ teaspoon cayenne pepper
1 tablespoon paprika
¾ teaspoon pepper
1 tablespoon chili powder or dry mustard
1½ cups catsup
2 tablespoons brown sugar
6 tablespoons hot water
20 frankfurters
20 hot dog buns

Blend vinegar and flour. Mix with onion, Worcestershire sauce, salt, cayenne pepper, paprika, pepper, chili powder or mustard, catsup, brown sugar and water. Pierce each frankfurter 5 to 6 times with fork and dip into sauce. Arrange in greased 13x9 inch baking dish and top with remaining sauce. Cover and bake at 350° for 1 hour. Serve with buns. *May be prepared ahead.*

Serves 10

Bacon and Cheese Dogs
Super for informal entertaining

Frankfurters
Cheddar cheese strips
Thick bacon slices
Hot dog buns (optional)

Split frankfurter lengthwise. Insert cheese, wrap with bacon and skewer with toothpicks. Place on broiler pan and broil for 5 minutes or until cheese is melted and bacon is crisp. Remove toothpick and drain. May be served on buns.

Serves 4 or 8

Mini Pizza

For the beginning chefs

Canned biscuits

Pizza sauce

Grated mozzarella cheese

Pepperoni slices

On greased baking sheet, flatten biscuits to 4 inch circles. Layer with pizza sauce, cheese and pepperoni. Bake at 425° for 10 minutes or until cheese is melted. *May be prepared ahead.*

Towering Pizza

A culinary marvel

1 pound ground beef

1 tablespoon oil for frying

2 tablespoons Worcestershire sauce

1 teaspoon onion flakes

¼ teaspoon pepper

¼ cup snipped parsley

16 canned crescent dinner rolls, divided

5 eggs, beaten

1½ cups grated Parmesan cheese

2 ounces diced pimiento

8 ounces provolone cheese, sliced

½ pound sliced cooked ham, divided

¼ pound sliced salami

8 ounces mozzarella cheese, sliced

3 ounces sliced cooked chicken

1 egg beaten

2 tablespoons water

Brown ground beef in oil and pour off grease. Add Worcestershire sauce, onion flakes, pepper and parsley, mixing well. Set aside to cool. Line 3 quart round baking dish with ½ of rolls to form bottom crust. Press seams together and extend dough 1 inch above dish. Blend 5 eggs and Parmesan cheese. Place ⅔ of mixture on crust. Sprinkle with pimiento and ground beef mixture. Layer with provolone cheese and ½ of ham. Cover with remaining egg and cheese mixture. Layer salami, remaining ham, mozzarella cheese and chicken. Use remaining rolls to form top crust, pinching edges with extended dough. Mix 1 egg with water and brush top crust. Bake at 350° for 1 hour or until brown. If edges brown too quickly, cover with foil and continue baking. *May be prepared ahead.*

Serves 10

123

Simple Supper Quiche

Effortless

12 ounces frozen spinach souffle, thawed
2 eggs, beaten
3 tablespoons milk
2 teaspoons chopped onion
½ cup sliced fresh mushrooms
½ pound Italian sausage, chopped
¾ cup grated Swiss cheese
1 (9 inch) pie crust

Mix spinach, eggs, milk, onion, mushrooms, sausage and cheese. Pour into crust and bake at 400° for 25 minutes or until done. For variation, ham or bacon may be used instead of sausage. *May be prepared ahead.*

Serves 6

Ham and Broccoli Quiche

What more do you need

10 ounces frozen chopped broccoli, cooked and drained
½ pound cooked ham, cubed
1 onion, chopped
4 cups grated Swiss cheese
½ teaspoon salt
¾ cup Bisquick
⅛ teaspoon pepper
½ teaspoon oregano
1 teaspoon parsley flakes
½ cup grated Parmesan cheese
4 eggs
½ cup salad oil
Grated Parmesan cheese (optional)

Combine all ingredients in large bowl and mix well. Pour into greased 10 inch pie plate. Bake at 350° for 35 minutes or until done. Cool for 10 minutes. Sprinkle with additional Parmesan cheese if desired before serving. *May be prepared ahead. May be frozen.*

Serves 6

Company Crab Bake

Makes entertaining a pleasure for the cook

2 cups mayonnaise

2 cups half and half

8 white bread slices, trimmed
   and cubed

12 to 16 ounces fresh or frozen
   crabmeat

12 eggs, hard boiled and sliced

4 ounces canned sliced
   mushrooms, drained

8 ounces sliced water chestnuts,
   drained

2 tablespoons minced onion

2 tablespoons chopped green
   pepper

2 ounces diced pimiento

¼ cup sherry

Crushed corn chips

Cooked rice (optional)

English muffins (optional)

In large bowl, blend mayonnaise with half and half. Add bread, stirring well. Mix in crabmeat, eggs, mushrooms, water chestnuts, onion, green pepper, pimiento and sherry. Transfer to greased 3 quart casserole. Cover and refrigerate overnight. Top with corn chips and bake at 325° for 1 hour. May be served over rice or English muffins. *Must be prepared ahead.*

Serves 10

Hot Crab Sandwiches
Satisfying luncheon menu

6 ounces canned crabmeat, drained

4 ounces cream cheese, softened

1 teaspoon minced onion

2 tablespoons mayonnaise

2 tablespoons catsup

½ tablespoon Worcestershire sauce

2 English muffins, halved and toasted

4 tomato slices

4 Old English cheese slices

In small bowl, blend crabmeat, cream cheese, onion, mayonnaise, catsup and Worcestershire sauce. On muffin, layer tomato, crabmeat mixture and cheese. Bake at 350° for 20 minutes.

Serves 4

Oyster Pies
Louisiana special

1 pint oysters with liquid

½ cup butter

2 large onions, sliced

2 shallots, chopped

2 celery ribs, chopped

3 garlic cloves, minced

2 tablespoons flour

2 bay leaves

½ teaspoon thyme

½ teaspoon Tabasco sauce

½ teaspoon salt

½ teaspoon pepper

Soft bread crumbs (optional)

12 patty shells

In saucepan, cook oysters over low heat until edges begin to curl. In stockpot, melt butter and saute onions, shallots, celery and garlic. Blend in flour and stir until thickened. Add oysters with liquid and mix well. Stir in bay leaves, thyme, Tabasco sauce, salt and pepper. Cook over low heat until thickened, stirring occasionally. For additional thickening, add soft bread crumbs. Warm patty shells and fill with oyster mixture. *For best results, prepare oyster mixture the day before. May be frozen.*

Serves 8

Baked Oysters and Artichokes

Tasty combination with class

6 tablespoons butter
1 1/4 cups seasoned bread crumbs
1/2 cup grated Parmesan cheese
1 tablespoon garlic powder
Salt to taste
Pepper to taste
14 ounces canned artichoke hearts, drained and chopped
6 tablespoons butter
1 tablespoon flour
3/4 cup milk
1 large onion, chopped
1 pint oysters with liquid, chopped

Melt 6 tablespoons butter in frying pan. Mix in bread crumbs, Parmesan cheese, garlic powder, salt and pepper. Stir in artichokes. Set aside. In saucepan, melt remaining butter and blend with flour and milk. Add onion and oysters with liquid, stirring well. Mix with artichoke mixture. Transfer to greased 1 1/2 quart baking dish. Bake at 350° for 45 minutes. *May be prepared ahead.*

Serves 8

Scallops and Artichokes au Gratin

Company entrees. . .one at a time

4 tablespoons butter

4 tablespoons flour

1 teaspoon salt

½ teaspoon pepper

1 cup milk

½ cup half and half

½ cup white wine

2 teaspoons Worcestershire sauce

1 pound scallops

6 ounces marinated artichoke hearts, drained and halved

4 ounces marinated mushrooms, drained

½ cup freshly grated Parmesan cheese

½ teaspoon paprika

In double boiler, melt butter and blend with flour, salt and pepper. Remove from heat and slowly stir in milk and half and half. Return to heat and stir continuously until thickened. Mix in wine and Worcestershire sauce. Place scallops, artichokes and mushrooms in individual gratin dishes. Cover with sauce and sprinkle with Parmesan cheese and paprika. Bake at 350° for 30 minutes. *May be prepared ahead and refrigerated. May be frozen.*

Serves 4

Baked Shrimp and Scallops
Seafood with influence

1½ pounds shrimp, peeled

½ pound scallops

½ cup soy sauce

½ cup butter, melted

1 tablespoon snipped parsley

6 garlic cloves, pressed

½ pound fresh mushrooms, thinly sliced

8 ounces sliced water chestnuts, drained

¼ pound fresh bean sprouts

Marinate shrimp and scallops in soy sauce for 30 minutes. In small bowl, mix butter, parsley and garlic. Set aside. Drain fish and transfer to 11x7 inch baking dish. Top with mushrooms, water chestnuts, bean sprouts and butter mixture. Bake at 350° for 30 minutes or until done. *May be prepared ahead.*

Serves 6

Shrimp Tetrazzini
Elegant when in a pasta mood

3 celery ribs, chopped

1 large onion, chopped

½ cup butter

1½ pounds shrimp, peeled

10 ounces cream of celery soup

10 ounces cream of mushroom soup

1 cup grated Cheddar cheese

¼ cup milk

½ teaspoon garlic powder

1 teaspoon Creole Seasoning

½ teaspoon salt

¼ teaspoon pepper

3 cups cooked egg noodles

In stockpot, saute celery and onion in butter. Mix in shrimp and cook until pink. Blend in soups, cheese, milk, garlic powder, Creole Seasoning, salt and pepper. Cook over low heat for 20 minutes. Stir in noodles and cook for 20 minutes. *May be prepared ahead.*

Serves 6

Spicy Shrimp over Rice

This deserves an encore

2 tablespoons chopped onion

1 garlic clove, minced

3 tablespoons butter

3 tablespoons flour

**1 tablespoon Worcestershire
    sauce**

½ tablespoon Tabasco sauce

1 teaspoon Accent

Salt to taste

1 cup whipping cream

¼ cup chili sauce

**1 pound shrimp, cooked and
    peeled**

2 cups cooked rice

In large frying pan, saute onion and garlic in butter. Blend in flour, Worcestershire sauce, Tabasco sauce, Accent and salt. Cook until thickened and bubbly. Stir in whipping cream and chili sauce. Mix in shrimp and heat. Serve over rice. *May be prepared ahead and may be frozen before adding shrimp.*

Serves 4

Scampi Aurora

Discovered in Venice, Italy

1 pound large shrimp, peeled

1 tablespoon lemon juice

2 tablespoons olive oil

½ teaspoon salt

½ teaspoon pepper

1 cup Hollandaise sauce

Arrange shrimp in shallow gratin dish. Sprinkle with lemon juice, olive oil, salt and pepper. Broil for 3 to 4 minutes on each side. Spoon warm Hollandaise sauce over shrimp and return to broiler for 2 minutes or until top is golden brown.

Serves 2

Shrimp Filled Artichokes

Luncheon main dish

6 artichokes

½ cup lemon juice

7 quarts water

⅔ cup salad oil

1 garlic clove, quartered

½ tablespoon salt

½ cup mayonnaise

½ cup sour cream

3 eggs, hard boiled and chopped

2 green onions, chopped

½ teaspoon dill

1½ tablespoons snipped parsley

½ teaspoon salt

8 ounces cooked and peeled small shrimp

Trim artichokes, tie with string from top to bottom, invert and dip in bowl of lemon juice. Set aside, reserving juice. In stockpot, add water, salad oil, 3 tablespoons reserved lemon juice, garlic and ½ tablespoon salt. Heat to boiling. Add artichokes. Bring to a boil, reduce heat and simmer for 30 minutes or until leaf easily pulls away from stalk. Remove artichokes, invert and drain. Refrigerate for at least 4 hours. Remove string and trim around heart. In large bowl, blend mayonnaise, sour cream, eggs, onion, dill, parsley and ½ teaspoon salt. Stir in shrimp and stuff into artichokes. *Must be prepared ahead.*

Serves 6

Shrimp and Artichoke Casserole

Fancy but convenient

14 ounces canned artichoke hearts, drained

1½ cups cooked rice

20 ounces cream of mushroom soup

1 small onion, chopped

2 pounds shrimp, cooked and peeled

2 cups grated Cheddar cheese

1½ garlic cloves, minced

2 tablespoons lemon juice

1 teaspoon cracked pepper

4 tablespoons butter, melted

1 tablespoon snipped parsley

½ cup grated Cheddar cheese

Green pepper slices

Arrange artichokes in greased 13x9 inch baking dish. In large bowl, mix rice, soup, onion, shrimp, 2 cups cheese, garlic, lemon juice, pepper, butter and parsley. Pour over artichokes and sprinkle with remaining ½ cup cheese. Bake at 350° for 30 minutes or until cheese is melted and mixture is bubbly. Garnish with green pepper. *May be prepared ahead. May be frozen.*

Serves 12

Baked Shrimp

For a 'you peel 'em' party

1 ½ cups butter, melted
⅔ cup lemon juice
1 tablespoon tarragon
8 ounces Italian salad dressing
5 pounds shrimp in shells

Mix butter, lemon juice, tarragon and salad dressing. Stir with shrimp in roasting pan. Bake at 350° for 40 minutes, stirring occasionally during baking.

Serves 8

Marinated Shrimp

A buffet triumph

2 large red onions, sliced
1 quart vinegar
1 cup salad oil
1 cup catsup
⅓ cup lemon juice
3 to 5 garlic cloves, pressed
½ cup sugar
1 tablespoon salt
1 teaspoon pepper
¼ teaspoon cayenne pepper
1 teaspoon paprika
½ teaspoon Tabasco sauce
2 tablespoons Worcestershire sauce
1 bay leaf
½ teaspoon chili powder
Capers to taste
5 pounds large shrimp, cooked and peeled

In large bowl, mix onions, vinegar, oil, catsup, lemon juice, garlic, sugar, salt, pepper, cayenne pepper, paprika, Tabasco sauce, Worcestershire sauce, bay leaf, chili powder and capers. Add shrimp and stir well. Cover and marinate in refrigerator for 3 days. Drain and serve in clear glass bowl. *Must be prepared ahead.*

Serves 8

Seafood Casserole Amandine

A recipe brought from France

1 celery rib, chopped

½ cup chopped green pepper

2 large onions, chopped

1 pound fresh mushrooms, sliced

Salt to taste

Pepper to taste

Garlic salt to taste

Oregano to taste

2 tablespoons butter

10 ounces cream of mushroom soup

2 pounds shrimp, cooked and peeled

6 ounces fresh or frozen crabmeat

2 cups cooked wild rice

2 cups cooked white rice

½ pound sharp Cheddar cheese, cubed

2¼ tablespoons butter, melted

2¼ tablespoons flour

1½ cups milk

¾ cup slivered almonds

2 tablespoons butter

In frying pan, saute celery, green pepper, onions, mushrooms, salt, pepper, garlic salt and oregano in 2 tablespoons butter. In large bowl, blend soup, shrimp and crabmeat. Add sauteed vegetables and wild and white rice, mixing well. Transfer to 3 quart baking dish, sprinkle with cheese and set aside. In small bowl, blend melted butter, flour and milk. Pour over casserole. Top with almonds which have been browned in 2 tablespoons butter. Bake at 325° for 50 minutes or until done. *May be prepared ahead.*

Serves 8

Sherried Seafood

Worth the expense for the compliments

6 tablespoons butter

7 tablespoons flour

3 cups milk

6 tablespoons dry sherry

1 1/4 teaspoons salt

1/8 teaspoon pepper

1 tablespoon Worcestershire sauce

12 ounces fresh or frozen crabmeat

1/2 pound shrimp, cooked and peeled

14 ounces canned artichoke hearts, drained

3 tablespoons lemon juice

1 cup grated sharp Cheddar cheese

In saucepan, melt butter and blend with flour. Gradually stir in milk. Cook until thickened. Stir in sherry, salt, pepper and Worcestershire sauce. Layer crab, shrimp and artichokes in greased 11x7 inch baking dish. Sprinkle with lemon juice and cheese. Top with sauce. Bake at 350° for 30 minutes. *May be prepared ahead.*

Serves 8

Sherried Flounder

Delicate flavor abounds

4 flounder fillets
1 cup sour cream
¼ cup sherry
Salt to taste
2 onions, sliced
Snipped parsley

Arrange flounder in 11x7 inch baking dish. Blend sour cream, sherry and salt. Pour over flounder and top with onions and parsley. Bake at 375° for 35 minutes.

Serves 4

Baked Sole Duxelles

First class buffet main dish

1 tablespoon olive oil
1 tablespoon flour
¼ pound fresh mushrooms, finely chopped
4 shallots, minced
¾ teaspoon tarragon
¼ cup snipped parsley
⅓ cup dry white wine or chicken broth
¼ cup whipping cream
6 sole fillets
Salt to taste
Pepper to taste
Paprika to taste
2 tablespoons butter
1 cup soft bread crumbs
¼ cup snipped parsley
1 cup grated Swiss cheese

In 13x9 inch baking dish, blend olive oil and flour. Spread over bottom of dish. In bowl, mix mushrooms, shallots, tarragon and ¼ cup parsley. Sprinkle in dish. Drizzle with wine then whipping cream. Lightly sprinkle fillets with salt, pepper and paprika. Arrange in baking dish and set aside. In small frying pan, melt butter, add bread crumbs and stir over medium heat until golden brown. Mix with remaining ¼ cup parsley and sprinkle over fish. Bake at 350° for 20 minutes or until flaky. Top with cheese and bake until cheese is melted. *May be prepared ahead before adding bread crumbs.*

Serves 6

Steamed or sauced, our selections are the cream of the crop

Asparagus in Cheese Sauce

Classy, outstanding vegetable

3 tablespoons butter

4 tablespoons flour

¾ cup milk

30 ounces canned asparagus spears, drained, reserving liquid

½ teaspoon Worcestershire sauce

Tabasco sauce to taste

Salt to taste

Pepper to taste

1 cup grated Old English cheese

¼ cup slivered almonds, toasted

¼ cup crushed potato chips

Melt butter in double boiler and blend with flour. Add milk, ¾ cup asparagus liquid, Worcestershire sauce, Tabasco sauce, salt and pepper, stirring well. Add cheese and stir until melted. Arrange asparagus in greased 11x7 inch baking dish. Sprinkle with almonds, add cheese sauce and top with potato chips. Bake at 325° for 30 minutes. *May be prepared ahead and refrigerated before baking.*

Serves 8

Curried Asparagus

Very delicate curry seasoning

2 tablespoons butter

2 tablespoons flour

½ cup half and half

1 cup chicken broth

¼ teaspoon curry powder

½ teaspoon lemon juice

¼ cup mayonnaise

2 eggs, hard boiled and chopped

30 ounces canned cut asparagus, drained

¼ cup crushed potato chips

In saucepan, melt butter and blend with flour. Slowly stir in half and half. Stir in chicken broth, curry powder and lemon juice. Cook over low heat until thickened, stirring continuously. Blend in mayonnaise and eggs. In greased 2 quart casserole, layer asparagus, sauce and chips. Bake at 400° for 20 minutes. *May be prepared ahead and refrigerated before baking.*

Serves 8

Baked Natural Asparagus

Ease and satisfaction guaranteed

1 to 1½ pounds fresh asparagus, trimmed
Salt to taste
Pepper to taste
3 tablespoons butter

Arrange asparagus in 1 quart shallow casserole. Sprinkle with salt and pepper and dot with butter. Cover and bake at 300° for 30 minutes.

Serves 4

Creole Green Beans

A Southern touch

8 bacon slices
32 ounces canned whole green beans, drained
1 tablespoon onion soup mix
16 ounces stewed tomatoes
1 teaspoon sugar

Fry bacon, drain, crumble and set aside. Reserve 3 tablespoons drippings in pan. Gently stir in beans and soup mix, heating thoroughly. Add ½ of bacon, stewed tomatoes and sugar, heat and mix well. Top with remaining bacon to serve. *May be prepared ahead.*

Serves 8

Jalapeno Green Beans

Lively flavored

6 ounces jalapeno pepper cheese
10 ounces cream of mushroom soup
64 ounces canned vertical pack whole green beans, drained
Bread crumbs

In double boiler, melt cheese and blend with soup. Gently stir in green beans. Transfer to greased 1½ quart baking dish. Sprinkle with bread crumbs and bake at 350° for 30 minutes. *May be prepared ahead.*

Serves 8

Gala Green Beans

Entertain with this casserole

8 ounces canned sliced mushrooms, drained
1 onion, chopped
½ cup butter
¼ cup flour
2 cups warm milk
3 cups grated sharp Cheddar cheese
⅛ teaspoon Tabasco sauce
2 teaspoons soy sauce
1 teaspoon salt
45 ounces frozen French style green beans, cooked and drained

In stockpot, saute mushrooms and onion in butter. Blend in flour, milk, cheese, Tabasco sauce, soy sauce and salt. Simmer until cheese is melted. Mix in green beans. Pour into 2 greased 13x9 inch baking dishes. Bake at 375° for 20 minutes. *May be prepared ahead.*

Serves 12

Overnight Green Beans

Sweet and sour flavor

5 to 6 bacon slices
2 eggs
¾ cup sugar
½ cup vinegar
32 ounces canned whole green beans, drained
8 ounces sliced water chestnuts, drained

Fry bacon, drain, crumble and set aside. Reserve ½ of drippings in frying pan. In bowl, blend eggs, sugar and vinegar. Stir into drippings and boil until thickened. Mix green beans and water chestnuts in 2 quart casserole. Pour egg mixture over beans, cover and refrigerate overnight. Sprinkle with bacon, cover and bake at 350° for 40 minutes. Uncover and bake for 5 minutes or until bacon is crisp. *Must be prepared ahead.*

Serves 6

Lemon Ring Green Beans

An attention getter

8 (¼ inch) lemon slices

32 ounces canned vertical pack whole green beans

With knife, cut an 'X' design in lemon pulp. Set aside. Divide green beans into 8 servings. Insert beans half way through 'X'. Transfer to shallow dish suitable for marinating. Pour dressing over beans, cover and refrigerate for 12 hours, basting frequently. *Must be prepared ahead.*

Serves 8

Dressing

⅓ cup sugar

1 teaspoon salt

1 teaspoon dry mustard

¾ cup salad oil

¾ cup vinegar

1 tablespoon celery seed

1 tablespoon minced onion

1 garlic clove, minced

Blend sugar, salt and mustard. Slowly add oil and vinegar, blending well. Stir in celery seed, onion and garlic.

Broccoli au Gratin

Good buffet dish

10 ounces frozen chopped broccoli

10 ounces cream of celery soup

¾ cup grated Cheddar cheese

¼ cup mayonnaise

¼ cup milk

½ cup Ritz cracker crumbs

2 tablespoons butter, melted

Cook broccoli, omitting salt, according to package directions. Drain and set aside. Blend soup and cheese. Separately blend mayonnaise with milk and stir into soup mixture. Place broccoli in 8 inch square baking dish and cover with sauce. Sprinkle with cracker crumbs and drizzle with butter. Bake at 350° for 45 minutes or until bubbly. *May be prepared ahead.*

Serves 6

Broccoli Pie

Popular with family and guests

2 cups chopped fresh broccoli
1 large onion, chopped
½ cup chopped green pepper
1 cup grated Cheddar cheese
1½ cups milk
3 eggs
¾ cup Bisquick
1 teaspoon salt
¼ teaspoon pepper

In saucepan, bring 1 inch salted water to a boil. Add broccoli, cook until tender and drain. Mix broccoli, onion, green pepper and cheese. Transfer to greased deep 10 inch pie plate. In bowl, blend milk, eggs, Bisquick, salt and pepper. Pour over broccoli. Bake at 400° for 35 minutes or until done. Let stand for 5 minutes before cutting. *May be prepared ahead.*

Serves 6

Sweet and Sour Brussels Sprouts

Tempt your family with this combination

8 bacon slices
2 tablespoons vinegar
1 tablespoon sugar
½ teaspoon salt
¼ teaspoon garlic powder
⅛ teaspoon pepper
3 cups fresh Brussels sprouts, cooked and drained

Fry bacon, drain, crumble and set aside. Reserve ¼ cup bacon drippings in pan. Stir in vinegar, sugar, salt, garlic powder and pepper. Add Brussels sprouts and mix until well coated and thoroughly heated. To serve, sprinkle with bacon.

Serves 6

Glazed Carrots and Grapes

A must for the holidays

4 tablespoons butter
2 teaspoons cornstarch
1/3 cup honey
1 teaspoon lemon juice
1/8 teaspoon cinnamon
8 carrots, sliced and cooked
1 cup seedless green grapes, halved

In small saucepan, melt butter and blend with cornstarch. Add honey, lemon juice and cinnamon. Cook, stirring continuously, until mixture boils. Gently mix with carrots and grapes. Serve immediately.

Serves 6

Carrots for Kids

. . .of all ages

1 pound carrots, sliced diagonally
2 tablespoons butter
2 tablespoons brown sugar
2 tablespoons corn syrup
2 tablespoons prepared mustard
1/4 teaspoon salt

In saucepan, simmer carrots in salted water for 20 minutes or until tender. Drain. In small saucepan, melt butter and blend with brown sugar, corn syrup, mustard and salt. Heat and pour over carrots, tossing gently until coated.

Serves 4

Italian Carrots

Zippy marinade

2 pounds carrots
1/2 cup salad oil
3/4 cup cider vinegar
3 small garlic cloves, pressed
1 teaspoon salt
1 tablespoon oregano

Parboil whole carrots for 2 minutes, thinly slice and set aside. Mix oil, vinegar, garlic, salt and oregano. Pour over carrots, cover and marinate in refrigerator overnight. Serve chilled or at room temperature. *Must be prepared ahead.*

Serves 8

Carrots in Cream and Dill

Makes carrots a winner

2 pounds carrots, julienned
2 large onions, sliced
1 garlic clove, minced
¼ cup olive oil
1 tablespoon flour
10 ounces cream of celery soup
1 cup milk
½ teaspoon dill
1 teaspoon sugar
Salt to taste
Pepper to taste
Allspice to taste

Saute carrots, onions and garlic in oil for 5 minutes. Sprinkle with flour and blend. Stir in soup, milk, dill and sugar. Simmer for 20 minutes or until carrots are tender, stirring occasionally. Mix in salt, pepper and allspice. *May be prepared ahead.*

Serves 6

Celery Casserole

For the vegetarian

8 celery ribs, coarsely chopped
1 onion slice
10 ounces cream of chicken soup
8 ounces sliced water chestnuts, drained
2 ounces diced pimiento
Pepper to taste
3 tablespoons butter
½ cup dry bread crumbs
¼ teaspoon salt
Slivered almonds

Cook celery with onion for 8 minutes in boiling water. Drain and discard onion. To celery, add soup, water chestnuts, pimiento and pepper. Pour into 1 quart baking dish. In small frying pan, melt butter, add bread crumbs and salt, browning slowly. Top celery with bread crumb mixture and almonds. Bake at 350° for 35 minutes. *May be prepared ahead, adding crumbs and almonds at baking.*

Serves 6

Baked Corn in Sour Cream

Robust for a cold day

6 bacon slices
2 tablespoons chopped onion
2 tablespoons flour
½ teaspoon salt
1 cup sour cream
24 ounces canned whole kernel corn, drained
1 tablespoon snipped parsley

Fry bacon, drain and crumble. Reserve 2 tablespoons drippings in frying pan. Saute onion in drippings. Blend in flour and salt. Gradually blend in sour cream. Stir in corn and ½ of bacon and heat for 2 minutes. Transfer to greased 1 quart baking dish. Bake at 350° for 15 minutes or until bubbly. Top with parsley and remaining bacon.

Serves 8

Corn Souffle

Cinnamon and sugar appeal to children

4 tablespoons butter
1 tablespoon sugar
1 tablespoon flour
½ tablespoon baking powder
½ cup evaporated milk
2 eggs, well beaten
24 ounces canned whole kernel corn, drained
Cinnamon sugar

In large frying pan, melt butter and stir in 1 tablespoon sugar. Blend with flour and baking powder. Gradually stir in milk and eggs. Fold in corn. Bake in greased 8 inch square baking dish at 350° for 40 minutes. Sprinkle with cinnamon sugar and serve.

Serves 8

146

Cabbage 'n Corn
A true Southern combo

5 bacon slices
1 tablespoon sugar
1 teaspoon salt
½ cup hot water
2 tablespoons vinegar
3 cups shredded cabbage
1 cup cut fresh corn

Fry bacon, drain, crumble and set aside. Reserve drippings in pan and mix with sugar, salt, water and vinegar. Heat to simmering and mix in cabbage and corn. Cover and cook for 7 minutes. To serve, sprinkle with bacon.

Serves 6

Fettuccini
Pasta lovers' favorite

1 cup butter
4 chicken bouillon cubes
8 shallots, chopped
1 cup whipping cream
¼ pound fresh mushrooms, sliced
Cracked pepper to taste
Tabasco sauce to taste
1 cup freshly grated Parmesan cheese
1 pound fettuccini, cooked and drained
Additional freshly grated Parmesan cheese

In double boiler, melt butter with bouillon cubes. Mix in shallots, whipping cream, mushrooms, pepper, Tabasco sauce and 1 cup Parmesan cheese. Simmer until mushrooms and shallots are soft and cheese is melted. Pour sauce over noodles, tossing gently. Garnish with additional Parmesan cheese. *Sauce may be prepared ahead.*

Serves 8

Mushrooms in Patty Shells

Fancy party vegetable

1 pound fresh mushrooms, sliced

2 tablespoons butter

1½ cups sour cream

¾ cup grated Parmesan cheese

3 tablespoons dry sherry

Garlic powder to taste

10 patty shells, baked

Parsley

In large frying pan, saute mushrooms in butter. Pour off liquid. Blend in sour cream, cheese, sherry and garlic powder, simmering until thoroughly heated. Spoon into patty shells. Garnish with parsley.

Serves 10

Onion Pie

Delicate flavor but hearty fare

1 cup cracker crumbs

½ cup butter, melted

6 large onions, thinly sliced

4 tablespoons butter

2 cups grated sharp Cheddar cheese

1½ cups milk

1 teaspoon salt

1 teaspoon pepper

2 eggs, beaten

Mix cracker crumbs and ½ cup butter. Press in bottom of deep 9 inch pie plate. Saute onions in remaining butter and spoon over cracker crust. Sprinkle cheese over onions. In saucepan, scald milk and add salt and pepper. Quickly mix in eggs and pour over cheese. Bake at 350° for 45 minutes or until golden brown.

Serves 8

148

Sweet Potato Casserole

Add turkey, pecan pie and family

29 ounces canned yams, mashed
1 cup sugar
½ teaspoon salt
½ cup butter, melted
1 teaspoon vanilla extract
1 cup brown sugar
½ cup flour
4 tablespoons butter, melted
⅛ teaspoon allspice
⅛ teaspoon cinnamon
1 cup chopped pecans

Mix yams, sugar and salt. Add ½ cup butter and vanilla, blending well. Pour into greased 1 quart baking dish. Mix brown sugar, flour, 4 tablespoons butter, allspice, cinnamon and pecans. Spread over yams. Bake at 350° for 20 minutes or until done. *May be prepared ahead.*

Serves 6

Potatoes Romanoff

A basic with gourmet flair

4 large potatoes
½ teaspoon salt
½ teaspoon pepper
1 cup sour cream
⅔ cup grated Cheddar cheese
4 green onions with tops, chopped
⅓ cup grated Cheddar cheese
½ teaspoon paprika
Butter

Cook potatoes in jackets until almost done. Peel and shred. Mix in salt and pepper. Blend with sour cream and ⅔ cup grated cheese and onions. Transfer to 1 quart baking dish, sprinkle with ⅓ cup cheese and paprika. Dot with butter and bake at 350° for 30 minutes or until brown. *May be prepared ahead.*

Serves 4

Potato Souffle

Visibly light and good eating

2 potatoes, cooked and peeled
2 to 3 tablespoons milk
8 ounces cream cheese, softened
2 eggs, lightly beaten
1 small onion, coarsely chopped
2 tablespoons flour
3 ounces canned French fried onion rings

With mixer, mash potatoes with milk until smooth. Add cream cheese, eggs, onion and flour. Beat at low speed until blended then on high speed until light and fluffy. Pour into greased 1 quart souffle pan and crumble onion rings on top. Bake at 300° for 35 minutes or until done.

Serves 6

Roasted Potato Fans

Simple but impressive

6 potatoes, peeled
6 tablespoons butter, melted
½ teaspoon salt
¼ teaspoon basil
¼ teaspoon marjoram
⅛ teaspoon pepper

Being careful not to cut all the way through, make slices every ¼ inch in potatoes. Pour butter into 13x9 inch baking dish. Arrange potatoes, cut side up, in dish. Brush with butter and sprinkle with salt, basil, marjoram and pepper. Bake at 400°, basting occasionally, for 1 hour or until potatoes are fanned and brown.

Serves 6

Jalapeno Baked Potatoes

Only in Texas

6 large potatoes
12 jalapeno peppers, halved
Shortening
Butter
Sour cream

Core 4 holes, 1 on each end and 1 on each side, in each potato. Stuff holes with jalapeno peppers. Lightly coat potatoes with shortening and separately wrap in foil. Bake at 450° for 1 hour. May be served with butter and sour cream.

Serves 6

150

Potatoes Florentine

Extraordinary

6 potatoes, cooked and peeled

½ cup butter

10 ounces frozen chopped spinach, cooked and drained

½ teaspoon salt

¼ teaspoon dill

¾ cup sour cream

Grated Cheddar cheese

Mash potatoes with butter. Blend with spinach, salt, dill and sour cream. Pour into 2 quart baking dish, sprinkle with cheese and bake at 325° for 15 minutes. *May be prepared ahead. May be frozen after cooking. To serve, thaw and reheat.*

Serves 8

Rice O'Brien

A flavor everyone will fancy

1 cup uncooked rice

1½ cups water

3 chicken bouillon cubes

1 teaspoon salt

1 tablespoon olive oil

1 bunch green onions, chopped

½ cup chopped green pepper

3 tablespoons diced pimiento

½ cup chopped ripe olives

½ cup butter

Mix rice, water, bouillon cubes, salt and olive oil in saucepan and bring to a boil. Cover and simmer for 20 minutes or until rice is done. In frying pan, saute green onions, green pepper, pimiento and olives in butter. Toss with rice. Transfer to greased 1 quart casserole, cover and bake at 350° for 20 minutes. *May be prepared ahead.*

Serves 8

Spinach Vera Cruz

Introduce this to the non spinach lover

10 ounces frozen chopped spinach

3 bacon slices

1 small onion, chopped

¾ cup sour cream

Tabasco sauce to taste

Salt to taste

Coarsely ground pepper to taste

½ cup grated Monterey Jack cheese

Thaw spinach, blanch in hot water and drain well. In frying pan, cook bacon, drain, crumble and set aside. Reserve 2 tablespoons drippings. Saute onion in drippings and blend in spinach, sour cream, Tabasco sauce, salt and pepper. Simmer slowly until thoroughly heated. Remove from heat and blend with cheese. Transfer to greased 1 quart baking dish, sprinkle with bacon and bake at 300° for 25 minutes. May also be used as a stuffing for tomatoes, topping with cheese, sour cream and bacon. *May be prepared ahead.*

Serves 4

Squash Amandine

Savory flavor

2 pounds fresh yellow squash, sliced

2 large onions, sliced

1 cup grated Cheddar cheese

2 eggs, beaten

2 tablespoons sugar

2 teaspoons salt

1 teaspoon pepper

½ cup butter, melted

1 cup cracker crumbs

⅓ cup slivered almonds

In saucepan, just cover squash and onions with water. Cook until tender and drain. Mix with cheese, eggs, sugar, salt and pepper. Pour into greased 1½ quart baking dish. Blend butter, crumbs and almonds and sprinkle on squash. Bake at 400° for 20 minutes or until done. *May be prepared ahead.*

Serves 8

Southern Squash

Tasting is believing

1 pound fresh yellow squash, sliced
1 small onion, coarsely chopped
2 tablespoons butter, melted
1 egg, lightly beaten
1 cup evaporated milk
½ teaspoon salt
1 cup grated Monterey Jack cheese
½ cup cracker crumbs

In saucepan, add squash, onion and just enough water to cover. Cover and cook for 10 minutes or until tender. Drain. Mix with butter, egg, milk and salt. Pour into greased 1½ quart baking dish and top with cheese and cracker crumbs. Bake at 350° for 30 minutes. *May be prepared ahead.*

Serves 6

Herb Squash

Substantial vegetable dish

2 pounds fresh yellow squash, sliced
1 small onion, chopped
Salt to taste
Pepper to taste
1 tablespoon butter, melted
10 ounces cream of chicken soup
1 cup sour cream
2 tablespoons diced pimiento
½ cup butter, melted
8 ounces herb seasoned stuffing mix

Cook squash and onion in water until tender. Drain. Blend with salt, pepper, 1 tablespoon butter, soup, sour cream and pimiento. Set aside. Mix ½ cup butter with stuffing. Stir ½ into squash mixture. Pour into greased 1½ quart baking dish and top with remaining stuffing. Bake at 375° for 30 minutes. *May be prepared ahead.*

Serves 8

Baked Tomatoes with Mushrooms

Arouses culinary interest

1 garlic clove, pressed

1 teaspoon minced fresh basil

1 tablespoon peanut oil

1 tablespoon butter

½ pound fresh mushrooms, chopped

Salt to taste

Pepper to taste

4 large tomatoes, halved

2 teaspoons sugar

½ cup dry bread crumbs

2 tablespoons peanut oil

In frying pan, saute garlic with basil in 1 tablespoon hot oil until brown. Add butter and heat. When hot, add mushrooms and stir over high heat for 2 minutes. Remove from heat, stir in salt and pepper and keep warm. Sprinkle each tomato with ¼ teaspoon sugar and additional pepper. Set aside. Mix bread crumbs with 2 tablespoons oil. Spread on tomatoes, place in 11x7 inch baking dish and bake at 425° for 20 minutes. Top with mushroom mixture.

Serves 8

Italian Tomatoes

Brighten up the menu

4 large tomatoes, peeled and halved

8 ounces Italian salad dressing

16 ounces marinated artichoke hearts, sliced

Dry bread or cracker crumbs

Basil

Grated Parmesan cheese

Butter

Place tomatoes in 11x7 inch baking dish. Pour dressing over tomatoes and refrigerate. One hour before serving, arrange artichokes over tomatoes. Sprinkle with crumbs, basil and cheese. Dot with butter and bake at 350° for 20 minutes. *Must be prepared ahead.*

Serves 8

154

Tomatoes Bergerette

Wonderful, different and tasty

8 tomatoes

½ teaspoon salt

**⅓ cup whipping cream,
whipped**

1 teaspoon Dijon mustard

3 green onions, minced

**2 tablespoons finely chopped
green pepper**

2 tablespoons snipped parsley

2 tablespoons diced pimiento

4 anchovy fillets, minced

1½ cups firm cooked rice

Parsley

Ripe olives

Slice tops off tomatoes. Remove pulp and reserve, discarding seeds and juice. Sprinkle shells with salt, invert and drain. Mix whipped cream, pulp, mustard, onions, green pepper, parsley, pimiento, anchovies and rice. To serve, spoon 1 teaspoon vinaigrette into each shell and fill with rice mixture. Garnish with parsley and ripe olives.

Serves 8

Vinaigrette

½ cup olive oil

3 tablespoons vinegar

½ teaspoon salt

⅛ teaspoon pepper

2 garlic cloves, minced

Mix all ingredients.

Tomato Pudding

Companion to roast beef

¾ cup boiling water

¾ cup brown sugar

½ teaspoon salt

10 ounces tomato puree

**3 white bread slices, trimmed
and cubed**

½ cup butter, melted

In saucepan, blend water, sugar, salt and tomato puree. Bring to a boil and continue boiling for 5 minutes. Place bread cubes in 1 quart casserole dish. Top with butter and tomato mixture. Cover and bake at 350° for 30 minutes. *May be prepared ahead.*

Serves 6

Italian Zucchini

Perk up a low calorie menu

1 pound zucchini, thinly sliced
Salt to taste
2 tablespoons olive oil
1 tablespoon butter
½ pound fresh mushrooms, sliced
2 green onions, chopped
Tomato slices
¼ teaspoon oregano
¼ teaspoon basil
3 tablespoons seasoned bread crumbs
Pepper to taste
1 cup grated mozzarella cheese

Arrange zucchini on paper towels and generously sprinkle with salt. Allow to stand for 1 hour and blot dry. In frying pan, heat olive oil and quickly brown zucchini. Transfer to greased 1 quart casserole. In frying pan, melt butter and saute mushrooms and onions for 5 minutes. Mix with zucchini and top with tomatoes. Sprinkle with oregano, basil, bread crumbs, salt, pepper and cheese. Cover and bake at 375° for 20 minutes. Uncover and bake for 15 minutes. *May be prepared ahead.*

Serves 6

Zucchini Bake

A combination men will love

4 to 5 zucchini, sliced
1 large onion, chopped
3 carrots, shredded
4 tablespoons butter
10 ounces cream of mushroom soup
4 ounces Cheese Whiz
2 cups seasoned croutons

Cook zucchini in water until done. Drain and set aside. In frying pan, saute onion and carrots in butter. Blend in soup and cheese. Fold in zucchini and croutons. Transfer to greased 1½ quart baking dish. Bake at 350° for 30 minutes. *May be prepared ahead.*

Serves 6

Zucchini Creole

New Orleans style

2 onions, chopped
1 small green pepper, chopped
3 celery ribs, chopped
¼ cup olive oil
28 ounces canned whole tomatoes
1 teaspoon basil
¼ teaspoon salt
1 bay leaf
Pepper to taste
3 to 4 zucchini, thinly sliced

In frying pan, saute onions, green pepper and celery in olive oil. Mix in tomatoes, basil, salt, bay leaf and pepper. Cover and simmer for 1 hour. Remove bay leaf and discard. Mix in zucchini. Cover and simmer for 1 hour. Uncover and simmer until thickened. *May be frozen after cooking and reheated.*

Serves 6

Zucchini Quiche

For brunch, too

1 cup Bisquick
2 tablespoons snipped parsley
½ teaspoon salt
½ teaspoon oregano
Pepper to taste
1 teaspoon garlic powder
4 eggs, beaten
½ cup salad oil
½ cup grated Parmesan cheese
2 onions, minced
4 zucchini, thinly sliced

Mix Bisquick, parsley, salt, oregano, pepper and garlic powder. In separate bowl, mix eggs, oil and Parmesan cheese. Combine with Bisquick mixture, stirring well. Stir in onions and zucchini. Place in greased 13x9 inch baking dish and bake at 350° for 25 minutes. Brown under broiler just before serving. *May be prepared ahead.*

Serves 8

Zucchini Fritters

A great way to serve your family zucchini

⅓ cup Bisquick
½ cup grated Parmesan cheese
2 eggs, beaten
2 zucchini, shredded
1 small onion, chopped
⅛ teaspoon pepper
2 tablespoons butter

Blend Bisquick, cheese, eggs, zucchini, onion and pepper. Melt butter over medium heat in frying pan. Using 2 tablespoons zucchini mixture for each fritter, spoon into frying pan and fry for 2 to 3 minutes on each side. Drain.

Serves 6

Crustless Vegetable Quiche

Ideal for the food processor

2 zucchini, sliced
½ pound fresh mushrooms, sliced
2 green onions, chopped
4 tablespoons butter
2 tomatoes, sliced
2 cups grated Monterey Jack cheese
1½ cups half and half
½ teaspoon salt
⅛ teaspoon pepper
1 tablespoon flour
3 eggs, beaten

In frying pan, saute zucchini, mushrooms and onions in butter. Drain and place in greased 11x7 inch baking dish. Top with layers of tomatoes and cheese. Beat half and half with salt, pepper, flour and eggs. Pour into baking dish. Bake at 375° for 40 minutes. *May be prepared ahead.*

Serves 4

Italian Vegetables

For the artichoke lover

28 ounces canned artichoke hearts
32 ounces canned French style green beans, drained
1 large onion, minced
½ cup olive oil
4 garlic cloves, pressed
1 cup seasoned bread crumbs
1 cup grated Parmesan cheese
¼ teaspoon salt
¼ teaspoon pepper
¼ teaspoon Tabasco sauce
½ cup dry bread crumbs
2 tablespoons butter, melted

Rinse, drain and mash artichoke hearts. Set aside. Rinse green beans with hot water and set aside. In large frying pan, saute onion in olive oil. Mix in garlic. Add beans and artichoke hearts. Cook and stir until thoroughly mixed. Add 1 cup bread crumbs, Parmesan cheese, salt, pepper and Tabasco sauce. Cook and stir until thickened. Transfer to greased 2 quart baking dish. Sprinkle with ½ cup bread crumbs and drizzle with butter. Bake at 350° for 20 minutes or until done. *May be prepared ahead.*

Serves 10

Grilled Vegetable Packets

Cookout fare. . .ready in a flash

2 chicken bouillon cubes
2 tablespoons water
3 tablespoons butter
½ teaspoon Accent
¼ teaspoon pepper
4 zucchini, sliced
2 tomatoes, coarsely chopped
1 onion, coarsely chopped
1 green pepper, sliced
Fresh mushrooms (optional)

In saucepan over low heat, dissolve bouillon cubes in water. Stir in butter until melted. Add Accent, pepper, zucchini, tomatoes, onion, green pepper and mushrooms, tossing until vegetables are well coated. Spoon mixture evenly into 6 foil squares. Wrap securely. Grill over medium heat, turning frequently, for 20 to 25 minutes. *May be prepared ahead.*

Serves 6

Very Special Fresh Vegetables

No words to describe it

1 pound zucchini, thinly sliced

1 pound carrots, thinly sliced

2 onions, thinly sliced

1 pound fresh yellow squash, thinly sliced

1 pound large fresh mushrooms, thinly sliced

Seasoned salt to taste

Pepper to taste

1 cup snipped parsley, divided

1½ cups grated Swiss cheese, divided

½ cup freshly grated Parmesan cheese, divided

12 cherry tomatoes, halved

Separately cook zucchini, carrots, onions, squash and mushrooms until tender but crisp. In 3 quart baking dish, layer zucchini, sprinkle with seasoned salt, pepper and parsley and top with Swiss then Parmesan cheeses. Repeat procedure with carrots then onions, squash and mushrooms. Arrange tomatoes on top and sprinkle with Parmesan cheese. Bake at 350° for 30 minutes. *May be prepared ahead.*

Serves 12

Noteworthy recipes that rise to the occasion

Quick Drop Biscuits
Magic before your eyes

1¼ cups self rising flour
1 cup whipping cream

In mixing bowl, blend flour with whipping cream. Drop by teaspoon onto greased baking sheet. Bake at 425° for 8 minutes or until done.

Serves 4

Corn Bread Muffins
Ranch favorite

2 cups flour
1½ cups corn meal
2 teaspoons salt
2 tablespoons baking powder
2 tablespoons sugar
2 cups milk
4 eggs, lightly beaten
½ cup salad oil
2 tablespoons honey

In large bowl, mix flour, corn meal, salt, baking powder and sugar. Set aside. In separate bowl, stir milk, eggs, oil and honey. Combine with flour mixture, stirring just until moistened. Fill preheated greased muffin tin cups with batter. Bake at 400° for 20 minutes or until done. *May be prepared ahead. May be frozen.*

Serves 12

Easy Cinnamon Crisps
An original

1 (10x3 inch) frozen puff pastry sheet, thawed
1 tablespoon cinnamon
¾ cup sugar
3 tablespoons butter, melted

Cut pastry into 3x¾ inch strips. Mix cinnamon and sugar and set aside. Dip pastry strips in butter then in cinnamon sugar mixture. Place 1 inch apart on baking sheet. Bake at 400° for 15 minutes or until crisp. Cool slightly before serving. *May be prepared ahead. May be frozen.*

Serves 4

Streusel Coffee Cake

Bakery treat from your oven

½ cup sour cream

½ cup buttermilk

¾ teaspoon baking soda

1 cup butter, softened

1 cup sugar

2 eggs

1 teaspoon vanilla extract

1½ cups flour

½ tablespoon baking powder

Blend sour cream, buttermilk and baking soda. Set aside for 45 minutes. With mixer, cream butter with sugar, add eggs then vanilla, mixing well. Set aside. Sift flour with baking powder. Add alternately with sour cream mixture to butter mixture. Mix batter well. Spread ½ of batter into greased 13x9 inch baking dish. Sprinkle with ½ of topping. Repeat layers. Bake at 350° for 30 minutes or until done. *Must be prepared ahead. May be frozen.*

Serves 8

Topping

¾ cup brown sugar

2 teaspoons cinnamon

¾ cup chopped pecans

Mix all ingredients.

Bishop's Bread

Welcome for new neighbors

5 eggs

1½ cups sugar

2½ cups flour

8 ounces chopped dates

1 cup chopped pecans

6 ounces semi sweet chocolate chips

1 tablespoon vanilla extract

With mixer, beat eggs until foamy. Slowly add sugar while beating at high speed. Reduce speed to medium and gradually add flour. Fold in dates, pecans, chocolate chips and vanilla. Pour into 2 greased 7x3 inch loaf pans. Bake at 350° for 45 minutes or until done. *May be prepared ahead. May be frozen.*

Serves 12

Plum Bread

Plumb good

2 cups flour
¾ cup sugar
1 tablespoon baking powder
1 teaspoon salt
½ teaspoon baking soda
½ teaspoon cinnamon
1 cup quick oats
32 ounces canned purple plums, drained and coarsely chopped
2 eggs, well beaten
1 cup milk
¼ cup salad oil

Mix flour, sugar, baking powder, salt, baking soda and cinnamon. Add oats and plums, stirring to coat. In separate bowl, blend eggs, milk and oil. Add to flour mixture, stirring just until moist. Pour into greased 9x5 inch loaf pan and bake at 350° for 1 hour or until done. Cool in pan for 10 minutes. *May be prepared ahead. May be frozen.*

Serves 8

Whole Wheat Banana Bread

Hearty after school snack

3 bananas, mashed
2 eggs
1 cup sugar
½ cup butter, melted
1 cup flour
1 teaspoon baking soda
½ teaspoon salt
1 cup whole wheat flour
⅓ cup hot water
½ cup chopped walnuts

With mixer, blend bananas, eggs, sugar and butter. In separate bowl, sift flour with soda and salt. Mix in whole wheat flour. Stir into banana mixture alternately with water. Mix on medium high speed for 2 minutes. Fold in walnuts and pour into greased 8x4 inch loaf pan. Bake at 325° for 1 hour and 10 minutes or until done. *May be frozen.*

Serves 8

Strawberry Bread with Spread

Holiday coffee special

3 cups flour

1 teaspoon baking soda

1 teaspoon salt

1 teaspoon cinnamon

2 cups sugar

1¼ cups salad oil

4 eggs, lightly beaten

20 ounces frozen strawberries, thawed and drained, reserving juice

In large bowl, mix flour, baking soda, salt, cinnamon and sugar. Make a hole in center and add oil, eggs and strawberries. Stir thoroughly by hand. Line 2 (8x4 inch) loaf pans with foil and pour in batter. Bake at 350° for 1 hour or until done. *Bread may be prepared ahead and frozen.*

Serves 12

Spread

½ cup reserved strawberry juice

8 ounces cream cheese, softened

Mix ingredients in blender.

Pear Bread

Moist and tasty

½ cup butter, softened

1 cup sugar

2 eggs

¼ cup buttermilk

2 cups flour

½ teaspoon salt

1 teaspoon baking powder

1 teaspoon nutmeg

1 cup chopped fresh pears

1 teaspoon vanilla extract

With mixer, cream butter and sugar. Add eggs, 1 at a time, beating well after each addition. Mix in buttermilk. Mix in flour, salt, baking powder and nutmeg. Fold in pears and vanilla. Pour batter into 4 greased 5x3 inch loaf pans. Bake at 350° for 45 minutes or until done. *May be prepared ahead. May be frozen.*

Serves 12

Zucchini Bread

Good toasted for breakfast

3 cups flour
2 cups sugar
2 teaspoons baking soda
1 teaspoon salt
¾ teaspoon nutmeg
½ tablespoon cinnamon
½ teaspoon baking powder
2 zucchini, shredded
8 ounces crushed pineapple
1 cup chopped nuts
1 cup salad oil
3 eggs, lightly beaten
1 cup raisins
2 teaspoons vanilla extract

In large bowl, mix flour, sugar, baking soda, salt, nutmeg, cinnamon and baking powder. Add zucchini, pineapple, nuts, oil, eggs, raisins and vanilla, blending thoroughly. Pour into 2 greased 8x4 inch loaf pans. Bake at 350° for 1 hour or until done. *May be prepared ahead. May be frozen.*

Serves 12

Apple Muffins

Even when apples aren't in season

3½ cups flour
2 cups sugar
1 teaspoon salt
1 teaspoon baking soda
1 teaspoon cinnamon
21 ounces apple pie filling, chopped
1½ cups salad oil
½ cup chopped pecans, toasted
1 teaspoon vanilla extract
Cream cheese (optional)

Combine all ingredients except cream cheese in large bowl, mixing only until blended. Spoon batter into greased muffin tin cups and bake at 350° for 20 minutes. May be served with cream cheese. *May be prepared ahead. May be frozen.*

3 dozen

Blueberry Tea Muffins

Zesty topping

½ cup butter, softened

1 cup sugar

2 eggs

1¾ cups flour

1 teaspoon baking powder

¾ teaspoon baking soda

¼ teaspoon salt

¼ teaspoon nutmeg

⅛ teaspoon cloves

¾ cup buttermilk

12 ounces canned blueberries, drained

¼ cup butter, melted

Topping

1 tablespoon grated orange peel

⅓ cup sugar

With mixer, cream ½ cup butter and 1 cup sugar. Add eggs, 1 at a time, beating well after each addition. Sift flour, baking powder, baking soda, salt, nutmeg and cloves. Add to butter mixture alternately with buttermilk, beating well after each addition. Fold in blueberries. Line miniature muffin tin cups with paper liners and fill ⅔ full. Bake at 375° for 20 minutes or until done. Dip muffins in melted butter then in topping mixture. *May be prepared ahead. May be frozen.*

4 dozen

Mix all ingredients.

Olive Bread

Moist version you'll want to bake

2 cups flour
½ cup sugar
4 teaspoons baking powder
1 teaspoon salt
¼ cup shortening
½ cup chopped nuts
¾ cup grated sharp Cheddar cheese
¾ cup stuffed olives, thinly sliced
1 egg, lightly beaten
1 cup milk
Cream cheese (optional)

Mix flour, sugar, baking powder and salt. Blend in shortening until coarsely crumbled. Fold in nuts, cheese and olives. Add egg and milk, stirring only until moist. Pour into greased 8x4 inch loaf pan. Let stand for 20 minutes then bake at 400° for 40 minutes or until done. May be served with cream cheese. *May be prepared ahead.*

Serves 8

Sausage Bread

Supper bread

1 pound hot sausage
1 large onion, chopped
¼ cup grated Parmesan cheese
½ cup grated Swiss cheese
1 egg, beaten
¼ teaspoon Tabasco sauce
½ tablespoon salt
2 tablespoons snipped parsley
2 cups Bisquick
⅔ cup milk
¼ cup mayonnaise
1 egg yolk, beaten

In frying pan, brown sausage with onion. Pour off grease. Mix in cheeses, egg, Tabasco sauce, salt and parsley. In bowl, blend Bisquick, milk and mayonnaise. In greased 8 inch square baking dish, layer ½ of batter, sausage mixture and remaining batter. Brush with egg yolk. Bake at 400° for 25 minutes or until done. *May be prepared ahead. May be frozen.*

Serves 4

Hot Herbed Bread

For the window sill gardener

1 loaf French bread

Cut bread into ½ inch slices. Lightly coat with butter mixture. In foil, reform bread into loaf. Cover and bake at 350° for 10 minutes. Uncover, fan bread and broil for 2 minutes or until golden brown.

Serves 6

Butter

1 cup butter

½ tablespoon rosemary

½ tablespoon thyme

½ tablespoon snipped parsley

1 teaspoon chopped onion

2 garlic cloves, pressed

Salt to taste

Coarsely ground pepper to taste

In saucepan, mix all ingredients. Heat until bubbly.

Herb Butter

Always on hand

2 cups butter, softened

1 tablespoon thyme

½ tablespoon snipped parsley

⅛ teaspoon garlic powder

½ teaspoon celery seed

Salt to taste

Blend all ingredients in small bowl. Cover and refrigerate for at least 6 hours. *Must be prepared ahead. May be frozen.*

2 cups

170

No Fail Refrigerator Rolls

Success is assured

½ cup warm water
1 teaspoon sugar
1 tablespoon dry yeast
½ cup shortening
1 cup milk
2 eggs
½ cup sugar
2 teaspoons salt
1 cup water
6½ to 7 cups flour

In large bowl, mix warm water with 1 teaspoon sugar, sprinkle in yeast and set aside to dissolve. In saucepan, mix shortening and milk. Cook over low heat but do not scald. In bowl, mix eggs, ½ cup sugar, salt and 1 cup water. Combine with shortening mixture. When lukewarm, mix with yeast. Gradually add flour, mixing until dough can be easily handled. Divide in ½ and place in greased bowls, turning to coat all over. Cover and refrigerate for 4 to 5 hours. Roll out on floured surface and shape into desired style of rolls. Let rise ½ hour and bake at 400° for 10 minutes for small rolls or 20 minutes for large rolls. *Dough must be prepared ahead. Rolls may be frozen after baking.*

4 to 5 dozen

Crusty French Bread

Rewarding for the whole family

1¾ cups milk
½ cup shortening
½ cup sugar
1 teaspoon salt
½ tablespoon dry yeast
¼ cup warm water
6 to 6½ cups flour
Corn meal for dusting
Melted butter

Scald milk and pour over shortening, sugar and salt in large bowl. Blend and cool to lukewarm. Dissolve yeast in water and mix with milk mixture. Blend in enough flour to make stiff dough. Cover and let rise in warm place for 1½ hours. Punch down and turn out on floured surface. Knead, adding flour, for 15 minutes or until dough is smooth and elastic. Divide into 2 parts. Roll each into 14x10x½ inch rectangle. Using long side, roll jelly roll style, pressing ends together. Grease and dust baking sheets with corn meal. Place loaves on sheets, brush with butter and allow to rise until doubled in size. Bake at 350° for 30 minutes. *Dough must be prepared ahead. Bread may be frozen.*

Serves 12

Caramel Sticky Rolls

Traditional Easter Sunday breakfast fare

1 tablespoon dry yeast
¼ cup warm water
1¾ cups milk
¼ cup sugar
½ cup butter
½ teaspoon salt
4 eggs, lightly beaten
7 to 8 cups flour
1¼ cups melted butter, divided

Soften yeast in water and set aside. Scald milk then mix in sugar and ½ cup butter. Cool to lukewarm. Stir in yeast and salt. Add eggs and beat. Place 7 cups flour in large bowl. Blend with milk and egg mixture. Mix in remaining flour, ¼ cup at a time, until dough forms a ball. Knead on floured surface for 5 minutes, adding additional flour if necessary, or until dough is smooth and elastic. Allow to set for 5 minutes. Roll into 36x12 inch rectangle. Spread ⅓ cup butter over center ⅓ of dough. Fold right ⅓ of dough over buttered section and coat top with ⅓ cup butter. Fold left ⅓ of dough over buttered section. Give folded dough a quarter turn and roll into ½ inch thick rectangle. Spread center ⅓ of dough with remaining ⅓ cup butter. Fold ends of rectangle to meet in center. Fold in ½, bringing edges together. Place dough in large greased bowl, cover and allow to rise in warm place for 1 hour or until nearly doubled. Punch down, cover and refrigerate for at least 4 hours. Split dough into 4 equal sections. Working with 1 section while remaining dough is refrigerated, roll into 12x9 inch rectangle, brush with 1 tablespoon butter and spread with ¼ of filling. Starting with long side, roll jelly roll style. Cut into 1 to 1½ inch slices. Repeat with remaining dough. Spread caramel topping in bottom of 4 (11x7 inch) greased baking dishes. Arrange dough slices over topping. Cover and let dough rise for 45 minutes or until doubled. Bake at 375° for 20 minutes or until golden brown. Cool 10 to 15 minutes before turning out. *May be partially baked and refrigerated or frozen.*

Serves 20

Filling

1½ cups sugar

1½ cups chopped nuts

2 to 3 teaspoons cinnamon

1½ cups butter, softened

Blend all ingredients.

Topping

1⅓ cups butter

2 cups brown sugar

½ cup corn syrup

In saucepan, combine all ingredients. Cook and stir until mixture is heated.

Christmas Morning Cinnamon Rolls

Start a Christmas tradition

½ cup milk

½ cup butter

½ teaspoon salt

⅓ cup sugar

½ tablespoon dry yeast

2 tablespoons warm water

1 cup flour

1 egg, lightly beaten

1¼ cups flour

6 tablespoons melted butter, divided

Red and green cherries

In large saucepan, scald milk and add ½ cup butter to melt. Add salt and ⅓ cup sugar, stirring until dissolved. Remove from heat. Dissolve yeast in water and stir into milk mixture. Blend in 1 cup flour. Add egg and beat for 2 minutes. Gradually blend in remaining flour. Turn out on floured surface and knead lightly 8 times. Place in greased bowl, cover and let rise until doubled. Roll dough into 20x8 inch rectangle. Spread 1 tablespoon melted butter over dough and sprinkle with ¼ of topping. Using long side, roll jelly roll style and cut into 25 pieces. Spread remaining melted butter in 11x7 inch baking dish. Place rolls, cut side up, in pan. Press on rolls to force butter up. Sprinkle with remaining topping. Press again. Allow to rise until doubled. Bake at 375° for 20 minutes. Arrange rolls to form Christmas tree. Garnish with red and green cherries. *Must be prepared ahead. May be frozen.*

Serves 12

Topping

1 cup sugar

½ cup brown sugar

1 tablespoon cinnamon

Mix all ingredients.

173

Double Duty Dough

Plays dual role

1 tablespoon dry yeast
½ cup warm water
1 teaspoon sugar
⅔ cup shortening
2 teaspoons salt
½ cup plus 2 teaspoons sugar
2 eggs
1 cup mashed potatoes, cooled
1 cup scalded milk, cooled
6 cups flour

Mix yeast, water and 1 teaspoon sugar and let stand in warm place for 10 minutes. With mixer, cream shortening, salt and ½ cup plus 2 teaspoons sugar. Beat in eggs then potatoes. Pour in milk, beating well. Mix in yeast mixture. Stir in flour, 1 cup at a time, until dough forms ball. Knead 12 minutes, adding additional flour if necessary, until dough becomes smooth and elastic. Shape into ball. Place in greased bowl and turn to coat all over. Cover and let rise in warm place for 1 hour or until doubled in size. Punch down.

Parker House Rolls

Dough
Melted butter

On floured surface, roll ¾ of dough ½ inch thick, reserving remaining dough for sticky buns. Cut with biscuit cutter, dip in butter and fold in ½. Place on greased baking sheet with sides touching. Cover and let rise for 1½ hours. Bake at 400° for 10 minutes or until done. Turn out on towel and cool.

6 dozen

Sticky Buns

Remaining dough
2 tablespoons butter, melted
½ cup sugar
2 teaspoons cinnamon
½ cup chopped pecans or raisins

Divide remaining dough and roll into 2 (12x8 inch) rectangles. Brush with butter. Mix sugar with cinnamon and sprinkle over dough. Using 8 inch side, roll jelly roll style and pinch sides to seal. Cut each roll into 8 slices and set aside. Spread topping on bottom of 2 (8x4 inch) loaf pans. Sprinkle with pecans or raisins. Place dough in pans and let rise for 1½ hours. Bake at 350° for 25 minutes or until done. Cool for 2 to 3 minutes before turning out of pan.

16 rolls

Topping

1 cup brown sugar
½ cup butter
2 tablespoons corn syrup

In saucepan, mix all ingredients over low heat, stirring continuously, until sugar is dissolved.

Butterscotch Pecan Rolls

Do ahead coffee cake

½ cup chopped pecans
18 frozen Parker House rolls
½ cup butter, melted
½ cup brown sugar
1 teaspoon cinnamon
4 ounces non instant butterscotch pudding mix

Sprinkle pecans in bottom of 10 inch greased tube pan. Arrange rolls in pan. Mix butter with brown sugar, cinnamon and pudding mix. Pour over rolls. Lightly cover and let stand at room temperature overnight. Bake at 350° for 25 minutes. Cool for 10 minutes before turning out. *Must be prepared ahead.*

Serves 8

Pineapple Delight

Complements pork

2 tablespoons cornstarch
¼ cup water
20 ounces canned crushed pineapple
2 eggs, beaten
1 teaspoon vanilla extract
½ to ¾ cup sugar
Cinnamon

Dissolve cornstarch in water. Mix with pineapple, eggs, vanilla and sugar. Pour into 1 quart baking dish. Sprinkle with cinnamon and bake at 300° for 1 hour.

Serves 6

Hot Sherried Fruit

Easy do ahead brunch

**16 ounces canned sliced
     pineapple, drained**

**16 ounces canned peach halves,
     drained**

**16 ounces canned pear halves,
     drained**

**16 ounces canned apricot
     halves, drained**

**15 ounces spiced apple rings,
     drained**

½ cup butter

3 tablespoons flour

½ cup brown sugar

**1 cup sherry or combined fruit
     juices**

Separately layer fruit in deep 2 quart casserole. In double boiler, melt butter and blend with flour, sugar and sherry. Heat and stir until smooth and thickened. While warm, pour over fruit, cover and refrigerate for at least 12 hours. Bake at 350° for 30 minutes. *Must be prepared ahead.*

Serves 12

Ladies' Delight

Delectable for a morning coffee

**12 ounces cream cheese,
     softened**

½ cup butter, softened

½ cup sour cream

½ cup sugar

1 envelope unflavored gelatin

¼ cup boiling water

¼ teaspoon grated lemon peel

½ cup white raisins

1 cup slivered almonds, toasted

Cinnamon graham crackers

In large bowl with mixer, blend cream cheese, butter and sour cream. Mix in sugar. Dissolve gelatin in water. Stir into cream cheese mixture along with lemon peel, raisins and almonds. Place in greased 1 quart mold and refrigerate until set. Serve with crackers. *Must be prepared ahead. May be frozen after unmolding.*

Serves 20

French Vanilla Toast
Family favorite

3 eggs, well beaten
½ cup evaporated milk
¼ cup sugar
½ teaspoon cinnamon
1 teaspoon vanilla extract
8 bread slices
Butter for frying

Mix eggs, milk, sugar, cinnamon and vanilla. Dip bread into mixture, coating both sides. Brown in butter in frying pan or on griddle, turning only once. *May be prepared ahead. May be frozen.*

Serves 4

Whole Wheat
Pancakes
Nutritious and delicious

2 cups flour
2 cups whole wheat flour
2 tablespoons baking soda
2 tablespoons sugar
1 quart buttermilk
6 eggs, beaten
1 tablespoon dry yeast
½ cup warm water
Blueberries (optional)

Mix flours, baking soda, sugar, buttermilk and eggs. Dissolve yeast in water and blend with flour mixture. Pour batter onto hot griddle and brown on both sides. Blueberries may be added while cooking. *May be prepared ahead.*

Serves 8

Chicken Crepes

Once tasted, often requested

4 eggs, beaten

½ cup plus 1 tablespoon flour

½ teaspoon salt

1½ cups milk

Oil for frying

2 tablespoons half and half

¼ cup grated Cheddar cheese

Freshly grated Parmesan cheese

Mix eggs, flour and salt. Add milk and blend. Heat ½ teaspoon oil in 5 inch crepe pan over medium high heat. Stirring batter each time, pour 2½ tablespoons or just enough batter to cover bottom of pan. Lightly brown on both sides. Remove to clean cloth and cool. Add 1 rounded tablespoon filling onto crepe, roll and place in greased 13x9 inch baking dish. Stir half and half into remaining white sauce. Spread over crepes. Sprinkle with Cheddar cheese. Top with Parmesan cheese. Bake at 350° for 20 minutes. *Crepes may be prepared ahead and stacked, covered and refrigerated or frozen if stacked with waxed paper between each crepe. Filling may be prepared ahead and frozen.*

Serves 8

White Sauce

6 tablespoons butter

6 tablespoons flour

½ tablespoon salt

3 cups chicken broth

In saucepan, melt butter and blend with flour. Mix in salt and slowly stir in chicken broth. Cook until thickened.

Filling

1 tablespoon snipped parsley

1 small onion, chopped

½ cup half and half

1 egg yolk

Sage to taste

Crumbled bacon to taste

¼ cup grated Cheddar cheese

3 cups cubed cooked chicken

Pepper to taste

In saucepan, simmer parsley and onion in half and half for 10 minutes. Mix with ½ of white sauce and slowly stir in egg yolk. Mix with sage, bacon, Cheddar cheese, chicken and pepper.

Easy Crab Quiche

Carefree entertaining

---

3 eggs, lightly beaten

---

1 cup sour cream

½ teaspoon Worcestershire sauce

¾ teaspoon salt

---

1 cup grated Swiss cheese

---

6 ounces canned crabmeat, drained

---

3 ounces canned French fried onion rings

---

1 (9 inch) deep dish pie crust, unbaked

Mix all ingredients except crust. Pour into crust and bake at 325° for 1 hour. *May be prepared ahead. May be frozen.*

Serves 6

Quiche Brotagne

A keen seafood selection

½ cup mayonnaise

---

2 tablespoons flour

---

2 eggs, beaten

½ cup white wine

---

6 ounces canned crabmeat, drained

---

3 ounces small cooked and peeled shrimp

---

2 cups grated Swiss cheese

---

1 small celery rib, sliced

---

5 green onions, chopped

---

1 (9 inch) pie crust, baked

Blend mayonnaise, flour, eggs and wine. Stir in crabmeat, shrimp, cheese, celery and onion. Pour into crust and bake at 350° for 35 minutes or until done. *May be prepared ahead. May be frozen.*

Serves 6

Tea Sandwiches
Really wonderful

8 ounces cream cheese, softened
2 tablespoons salad dressing
1 teaspoon lemon juice
¼ teaspoon seasoned salt
8 carrots, finely shredded
1½ pounds whole wheat sandwich bread, trimmed

With mixer, blend cream cheese, salad dressing, lemon juice and seasoned salt. Fold in carrots. Spread on bread, top with another slice bread and quarter. *May be prepared ahead.*

Serves 12

Baked Chicken Sandwich
Epitome of sandwiches

2 cups chopped cooked chicken
12 ounces chicken gravy
2 teaspoons chopped onion
10 ounces cream of mushroom soup
2 teaspoons diced pimiento
8 ounces sliced water chestnuts, drained
24 white bread slices, trimmed
4 eggs, beaten
2 tablespoons milk
Crushed potato chips
Hollandaise sauce

Mix chicken with gravy, onion, soup, pimiento and water chestnuts. Spread mixture onto 12 bread slices and top with remaining bread. Wrap and freeze. When ready to use, beat eggs with milk. Dip frozen sandwich in egg mixture then in chips. Place on greased baking sheet and bake at 300° for 1 hour or until lightly brown. Serve with Hollandaise sauce. *Must be prepared ahead.*

Serves 12

Ham and Swiss Sandwich Puff

Good for leftover ham

2 cups ground cooked ham

2 cups grated Swiss cheese

½ cup mayonnaise

1 teaspoon prepared mustard

12 white bread slices, toasted

6 eggs

2¼ cups milk

Parsley

Mix ham and cheese in bowl. Blend in mayonnaise and mustard. Spread on 6 toast slices and top with remaining toast. Cut each diagonally into quarters. Stand, crust edge down, in greased 13x9 inch baking dish. Beat eggs slightly with milk and pour over sandwiches. Cover and refrigerate for at least 4 hours. Bake at 325° for 35 minutes or until custard sets. Garnish with parsley. *Must be prepared ahead.*

Serves 6

Ham and Broccoli Strata

A meal in a jiffy

12 white bread slices, trimmed

3 cups grated sharp Cheddar cheese, divided

20 ounces frozen chopped broccoli, cooked and drained

3 cups cubed cooked ham

3 cups milk

6 eggs, beaten

½ teaspoon salt

¼ teaspoon dry mustard

Onion flakes

In greased 13x9 inch baking dish, layer 6 bread slices, 1 cup cheese, remaining slices, 1 cup cheese, broccoli, ham, and remaining 1 cup cheese. In bowl, mix milk, eggs, salt and mustard. Pour over casserole and sprinkle with onion. Cover and refrigerate for at least 6 hours. Remove from refrigerator 1 hour before baking. Bake at 325° for 1 hour. Let stand for 10 minutes before serving. *Must be prepared ahead.*

Serves 8

Sausage and Egg Strata

Great buffet selection

2 pounds sausage, browned and drained
3 green onions, chopped
1 teaspoon dry mustard
Salt to taste
Pepper to taste
16 firm white bread slices, trimmed
6 eggs, beaten
3 cups milk
2 teaspoons Worcestershire sauce
1 cup grated Cheddar cheese

Mix sausage, onion, mustard, salt and pepper. In greased 13x9 inch baking dish, layer 8 bread slices, sausage mixture and remaining slices. In bowl, mix eggs with milk and Worcestershire sauce. Pour over casserole. Cover and refrigerate overnight. Place baking dish in larger ovenproof pan filled with 1 inch water. Loosely cover and bake at 325° for 1 hour. Remove baking dish from water, uncover, sprinkle with cheese and bake for 15 minutes. *Must be prepared ahead.*

Serves 8

Sausage 'n Spuds Omelet

Hearty way to start your husband's day

2 tablespoons butter
¾ cup frozen hash brown potatoes, thawed
3 tablespoons chopped onion
3 tablespoons chopped green pepper
¾ cup chopped Polish sausage
½ teaspoon basil
½ teaspoon salt
⅛ teaspoon pepper
4 eggs
1 tablespoon water
2 tablespoons butter

In frying pan, melt 2 tablespoons butter. Add potatoes and cook for 5 minutes or until golden brown. Mix in onion, green pepper, sausage, basil, salt and pepper. Cook until vegetables are tender. Remove from heat and set aside. Beat eggs with water. In another large frying pan, melt remaining 2 table-spoons butter. Add egg mixture and cook over low heat, without stirring, until eggs are set. Spoon potato and sausage mixture over 1/2 of eggs and fold. Heat and serve.

Serves 2

Sausage and Cheese Grits

Splendid family breakfast

¹⁄₂ cup butter, softened
6 ounces garlic cheese, cubed
1 cup quick grits, prepared
2 eggs, lightly beaten
Milk
1 pound sausage, well browned and drained

In large bowl, mix butter and cheese with warm grits. Beat eggs in measuring cup and add enough milk to equal 1 cup. Mix with grits. Stir sausage into grits mixture. Transfer to greased 1½ quart baking dish. Bake at 350° for 1 hour. *May be prepared ahead. May be frozen before baking.*

Serves 6

Frosted Egg Mold

Unusual brunch appetizer

8 eggs, hard boiled and finely chopped
¹⁄₂ cup butter, melted
1 teaspoon minced green onion
³⁄₄ teaspoon salt
¹⁄₈ teaspoon pepper
¹⁄₈ teaspoon curry powder
¹⁄₃ cup sour cream
Chopped chives
Parsley
Crackers

Combine eggs, butter, onion, salt, pepper and curry powder, mixing well. Spoon into greased 4 cup mold, cover and refrigerate for 3 hours or until set. Unmold, spread with sour cream and sprinkle with chives and parsley. Serve with crackers. *Must be prepared ahead.*

Serves 12

Stuffed Eggs au Gratin

A stimulating choice

6 eggs, hard boiled

4 tablespoons butter, melted

½ teaspoon Worcestershire sauce

¼ teaspoon prepared mustard

2 ounces canned deviled ham

3 green onions, chopped

1 tablespoon snipped parsley

Salt to taste

Pepper to taste

1 cup grated Cheddar cheese

¼ cup dry bread crumbs

Sauce

4 tablespoons butter

¼ cup flour

2 cups milk

2 teaspoons chopped chives

1 teaspoon salt

¼ teaspoon pepper

Cut eggs in ½ lengthwise and scoop yolks into small bowl. Mix yolks with butter, Worcestershire sauce, mustard, ham, onions, parsley, salt and pepper. Stuff egg whites and arrange in greased 8 inch square baking dish. Pour sauce over eggs. Sprinkle with cheese and top with bread crumbs. Bake at 325° for 25 minutes or until done. *May be prepared a day ahead, adding sauce at baking time.*

Serves 6

In saucepan, melt butter and blend with flour. Add milk, chives, salt and pepper. Simmer, stirring frequently, until mixture is thickened.

Sweet ideas for pleasing kids 'n company

Easy Pecan Loaf

A holiday favorite you'll remember

3 cups pecan halves

1 cup chopped dates

1 cup maraschino cherries

¾ cup flour

¾ cup sugar

½ teaspoon salt

3 eggs, well beaten

1 teaspoon vanilla extract

In large bowl, place pecans, dates and cherries. Sift flour, sugar and salt over mixture and toss well. Stir in eggs and vanilla. Press into greased 9x5 inch loaf pan and bake at 300° for 1 hour and 45 minutes. *May be prepared ahead. May be frozen.*

Serves 12

Waxy Pecan Cake

Great substitute for fruit cake

6 egg whites

1 pound brown sugar

2 cups flour, sifted

1 teaspoon baking powder

1 tablespoon water

3 cups chopped pecans

1 teaspoon vanilla extract

Whipped cream

Place all ingredients except whipped cream in large bowl and stir gently until well blended. Pour batter into greased and floured 10 inch tube pan. Remove air bubbles. Place in cold oven. Bake at 350° for 1 hour. Serve with whipped cream. *May be prepared ahead. May be frozen.*

Serves 12

Five Flavor Pound Cake

Smells fantastic while baking

3 cups sugar
1 cup butter, softened
½ cup shortening
5 eggs
3 cups flour, sifted
½ teaspoon baking powder
1 cup milk
1 teaspoon coconut extract
1 teaspoon lemon extract
1 teaspoon rum extract
1 teaspoon vanilla extract
1 teaspoon butter flavoring

With mixer, cream sugar, butter and shortening. Beat in eggs, 1 at a time. Slowly blend in flour and baking powder. Mix in milk, extracts and flavoring. Pour batter into greased 10 inch tube pan and bake at 325° for 1½ hours. Glaze while warm. *May be prepared ahead. May be frozen.*

Serves 12

Glaze

½ teaspoon coconut extract
½ teaspoon lemon extract
½ teaspoon vanilla extract
½ teaspoon almond extract
½ teaspoon butter flavoring
1 cup sugar
½ cup water

Mix all ingredients in saucepan. Heat to boiling.

Cream Cheese Pound Cake

Disappears before your eyes

1½ cups butter, softened
3 cups sugar
8 ounces cream cheese, softened
6 eggs
1 teaspoon vanilla extract
3 cups flour

With mixer, cream butter, sugar and cream cheese. Beat in eggs, 1 at a time. Blend in vanilla and flour. Pour batter into greased 10 inch tube pan. Place in cold oven. Bake at 300° for 2 hours without opening oven door during baking time. *May be prepared ahead. May be frozen.*

Serves 12

Vanilla Wafer Pound Cake

Quickly mixed and welcomed any time

1 cup butter, softened
6 eggs
3 ounces canned shredded coconut
12 ounces vanilla wafers, crushed
2 cups sugar
½ cup milk
1 cup chopped pecans

Combine all ingredients and mix well. Bake in greased 10 inch tube pan at 350° for 1 hour or until golden brown. *May be prepared ahead. May be frozen.*

Serves 12

Amaretto Cheesecake

A masterpiece

¼ cup plus 2 tablespoons butter, melted

1½ cups graham cracker crumbs

2 tablespoons sugar

1 teaspoon cinnamon

24 ounces cream cheese, softened

1 cup sugar

4 eggs

⅓ cup Amaretto

¼ cup slivered almonds, toasted

12 ounces chocolate candy bars, grated

Mix butter, crumbs, 2 tablespoons sugar and cinnamon. Press into bottom and ½ inch up sides of 9 inch springform pan. Beat cream cheese with mixer until light and fluffy. Gradually mix in 1 cup sugar. Add eggs, 1 at a time, beating well after each addition. Stir in Amaretto then pour into pan. Bake at 375° for 45 minutes or until set. Spread on topping. Bake at 500° for 5 minutes. Cool to room temperature. Refrigerate for at least 24 hours. Garnish with almonds and chocolate. *Must be prepared ahead.*

Serves 12

Topping

1 cup sour cream

4 teaspoons sugar

1 tablespoon Amaretto

Blend all ingredients.

Traditional Cheesecake

Top with one of our sauces

½ cup butter, melted
1⅔ cups graham cracker crumbs
½ cup sugar
48 ounces cream cheese, softened
6 eggs
½ cup plus 2 tablespoons flour
1½ cups whipping cream
1 teaspoon vanilla extract
½ teaspoon lemon juice
2½ cups sugar

Mix butter, crumbs and ½ cup sugar. Press into bottom of 12 inch springform pan. With mixer, blend cream cheese, eggs, flour, whipping cream, vanilla, lemon juice and remaining 2½ cups sugar. Spread over crust. Place springform pan in larger ovenproof pan filled with 1 inch water. Bake at 350° for 1 hour. Turn oven off and let cake remain with door closed for 1 hour. Remove, cool to room temperature then chill. *Must be prepared ahead. May be frozen in springform pan and thawed 24 hours before serving.*

Serves 12

Blackberry Wine Cake

Serve with coffee in front of a roaring fire

18 ounces deluxe yellow cake mix
3 ounces blackberry gelatin
4 eggs, beaten
½ cup salad oil
1 cup blackberry wine
1 cup chopped pecans

Stir cake mix and gelatin. Blend in eggs, oil and wine. Grease and heavily flour 10 inch tube pan. Sprinkle pecans in bottom and pour in batter. Bake at 325° for 45 minutes or until done. Cool and glaze. *Must be prepared ahead.*

Serves 12

Glaze

½ cup butter
½ cup blackberry wine
1 cup confectioners' sugar

Heat and blend butter and wine. Stir in sugar until dissolved.

191

Butternut Cake

Fantastic gourmet cake

18 ounces butter flavored yellow cake mix

¾ cup salad oil

½ cup sugar

5 eggs

1 teaspoon vanilla extract

1 cup sour cream

1 cup chopped nuts

1 teaspoon cinnamon

1 teaspoon brown sugar

Frosting

½ cup butter, softened

6 ounces cream cheese, softened

1 pound confectioners' sugar

1 teaspoon vanilla extract

1 cup chopped nuts

Blend cake mix, oil, sugar, eggs, vanilla and sour cream. Stir in nuts. Pour ½ into greased and floured 10 inch tube pan. Mix cinnamon and brown sugar and sprinkle over batter. Top with remaining batter. Bake at 350° for 1 hour. Cool and frost. *May be prepared ahead. May be frozen.*

Serves 12

With mixer, cream butter, cream cheese and confectioners' sugar. Mix in vanilla and nuts.

Yummy Coconut Cake

Freezes well if it lasts

18 ounces white or yellow cake mix
¼ cup salad oil
3 eggs
1 cup sour cream
8 ounces cream of coconut
Shredded coconut

With mixer, beat cake mix, oil, eggs, sour cream and cream of coconut on low speed for 1 minute. Beat on medium speed for 2 to 3 minutes. Pour into greased and floured 13x9 inch baking dish. Bake at 350° for 25 minutes or until done. Cool and frost. Garnish with shredded coconut. *May be prepared ahead. May be frozen.*

Serves 12

Frosting

8 ounces cream cheese, softened
2 tablespoons milk
1 pound confectioners' sugar, sifted

Blend all ingredients with mixer.

Mocha Mousse Cake

From a Santa Fe restaurant

12 ounces semi sweet chocolate chips
2 tablespoons instant coffee granules
3 tablespoons water
2 tablespoons sugar
1 teaspoon vanilla extract
7 eggs, separated
8 ounces chocolate wafers, crushed
Whipped cream

Combine chocolate chips, coffee, water, sugar and vanilla in double boiler. Stir and cook until well heated. Cool. Beat with mixer then beat in egg yolks. Set aside. Beat egg whites until stiff. Fold into chocolate mixture. Press ⅓ of wafers in 11x7 inch dish. Top with ½ of chocolate mixture. Repeat wafer and chocolate layers. Top with remaining wafers. Chill. Garnish with whipped cream. *Must be prepared ahead.*

Serves 12

Triple Chocolate Cake

For the chocoholic

18 ounces deep chocolate cake mix

4 ounces chocolate instant pudding mix

¾ cup sour cream

½ cup salad oil

½ cup water

½ cup chopped almonds, toasted

¼ cup mayonnaise

4 eggs

3 tablespoons Amaretto

1 teaspoon almond extract

1 cup semi sweet chocolate chips

1 tablespoon cocoa for dusting

Glaze

1 cup confectioners' sugar

3 tablespoons milk

1 teaspoon almond extract

Place cake mix, pudding mix, sour cream, oil, water, almonds, mayonnaise, eggs, Amaretto and almond extract in large bowl. With mixer, beat for 2 minutes on medium speed. Fold in chocolate chips. Grease 10 inch tube pan and dust with cocoa. Pour batter into pan and bake at 350° for 50 minutes or until done. Cool on cake rack for 10 minutes. Drizzle warm cake with glaze. *May be prepared ahead. May be frozen.*

Serves 12

Mix all ingredients in small bowl. Let stand at room temperature until ready for use.

Mexican Chocolate Cake with Praline Frosting

A strong competitor for first place

1 cup boiling water
3 ounces unsweetened chocolate
½ cup butter, softened
1 teaspoon vanilla extract
1¾ cups brown sugar
2 eggs
1¾ cups plus 2 tablespoons flour
1 teaspoon baking soda
¼ teaspoon salt
½ cup sour cream
½ cup finely chopped pecans

Pour water over chocolate in bowl. Stir to melt and set aside to cool. With mixer, cream butter and vanilla, add brown sugar and blend well. Beat in eggs, 1 at a time. Sift flour, soda and salt into creamed mixture and mix well. Blend in sour cream and chocolate mixture. Pour into greased 9x5 inch loaf pan. Bake at 350° for 1 hour and 15 minutes. Cool for 10 minutes and frost. Garnish with pecans. *May be prepared ahead.*

Serves 12

Frosting

½ cup butter
1 cup brown sugar
¼ cup milk
1 to 2 cups confectioners' sugar, sifted
½ teaspoon vanilla extract

Blend butter and brown sugar in saucepan. Boil over medium heat for 2 minutes, stirring continuously. Add milk and bring to a boil. Remove from heat and cool to lukewarm. Gradually stir in sugar until frosting reaches desired consistency. Mix in vanilla.

Chocolate Eclair Cake

Divine dessert in the freezer

1 pound graham crackers

8 ounces French vanilla instant pudding mix

3 cups milk

8 ounces frozen whipped topping, thawed

Layer bottom of greased 13x9 inch dish with ⅓ of graham crackers. Beat pudding mix with milk and fold in whipped topping. Spread ½ over graham crackers. Repeat layers, ending with graham crackers. Frost and refrigerate for 24 hours. *Must be prepared ahead. May be frozen.*

Serves 24

Frosting

2 ounces unsweetened liquid chocolate

3 tablespoons butter, softened

2 tablespoons milk

1 teaspoon vanilla extract

1½ cups confectioners' sugar

Blend chocolate, butter, milk and vanilla. Stir in confectioners' sugar until smooth.

Delicious Chocolate Chip Cake

Marvelous cake that needs no icing

18 ounces butter flavored yellow cake mix

4 ounces vanilla instant pudding mix

¾ cup salad oil

4 eggs

1 cup sour cream

1 teaspoon vanilla extract

6 ounces semi sweet chocolate chips

5 ounces chocolate syrup

Combine cake mix, pudding mix, oil, eggs, sour cream and vanilla, beating until well mixed. Pour ½ into greased and floured 10 inch tube pan. To remaining mixture, add chocolate chips and syrup. Mix well. Pour into pan and bake at 350° for 1 hour. *May be prepared ahead.*

Serves 12

Orange Glazed Carrot Cake

A perennial favorite

4 eggs, beaten

2 cups sugar

1 1/4 cups salad oil

1 teaspoon vanilla extract

2 cups flour

2 teaspoons baking soda

2 teaspoons baking powder

1 teaspoon salt

1 teaspoon cinnamon

1/4 cup buttermilk

3 tablespoons grated orange peel

1 cup chopped pecans

1 pound carrots, shredded

Glaze

8 ounces cream cheese, softened

1 pound confectioners' sugar

Orange juice

Beat eggs with sugar, oil and vanilla. Sift flour, baking soda, baking powder, salt and cinnamon and mix with egg mixture. Stir in buttermilk. Fold in orange peel, pecans and carrots. Pour into greased and floured 10 inch tube pan and bake at 350° for 30 minutes or until done. Cool and glaze. *Must be prepared ahead.*

Serves 12

With mixer, blend cream cheese and sugar, gradually stirring in orange juice until glaze reaches desired consistency.

Mandarin Orange Cake

Company cake in a jif

18 ounces butter flavored yellow cake mix

4 eggs

1 cup salad oil

11 ounces canned mandarin oranges

Combine cake mix with eggs and stir by hand until mixed. Stir in oil. Fold in oranges. Pour into 3 greased and floured 9 inch cake pans and bake at 350° for 15 minutes or until done. Cool and frost. *May be prepared ahead.*

Serves 12

Frosting

20 ounces canned crushed pineapple, drained

4 ounces vanilla instant pudding mix

8 ounces frozen whipped topping, thawed

Mix pineapple and pudding mix then fold in topping.

Sweetheart Strawberry Cake

Beautiful. . .not only for Valentine's

18 ounces white cake mix

4 eggs

1 cup salad oil

3 ounces strawberry gelatin

10 ounces frozen strawberries

With mixer, beat cake mix with eggs, oil, gelatin and strawberries for 4 minutes. Pour into 3 greased and floured 8 inch round cake pans. Bake at 350° for 30 minutes or until done. Cool, frost and refrigerate for at least 2 hours before serving. *Must be prepared ahead.*

Serves 12

Frosting

2 cups whipping cream

2 tablespoons sugar

10 ounces frozen strawberries, thawed and drained

With mixer, whip cream and sugar then fold in strawberries.

Pineapple Sheet Cake

Old fashioned standby renewed

2 eggs, beaten
2 cups sugar
2 cups flour
2 teaspoons vanilla extract
2 teapoons baking soda
12 ounces canned crushed pineapple

Combine all ingredients and mix well. Pour into greased and floured 17x11 inch jelly roll pan. Bake at 350° for 30 minutes. Frost while hot. *May be prepared ahead.*

Serves 12

Frosting

4 tablespoons butter, softened
3 ounces cream cheese, softened
2 cups confectioners' sugar, sifted
1 teaspoon vanilla extract
1 cup chopped pecans

With mixer, cream butter and cream cheese. Blend in confectioners' sugar and vanilla. Stir in pecans. Keep warm until ready to use.

Almond Cake

A rich, sophisticated dessert

2 cups butter, softened
1½ cups sugar
2 eggs, separated
7 ounces soft almond paste
2 teaspoons almond extract
4 cups flour
1 cup sliced almonds

Beat butter and sugar with mixer at medium speed until light and fluffy. Beat in egg yolks then almond paste and almond extract. At low speed, beat in flour just until smooth. Press into 13x9 inch baking dish. Beat egg whites until foamy and brush over dough. Sprinkle with almonds and bake at 350° for 30 minutes. Cool to cut. *May be prepared ahead. May be frozen.*

Serves 12

Forgotten Cake

A make ahead birthday cake, leaving time for buying present

18 ounces yellow cake mix, mixed

2 cups sour cream

2 cups canned shredded coconut

2 cups sugar

12 ounces frozen whipped topping, thawed

Pour batter into 2 (9 inch) round cake pans. Adding 5 minutes to cooking time, bake according to package directions. Cool and split each cake into 2 layers. Blend sour cream, coconut and sugar. Reserving ¾ cup, spread sour cream mixture on top of 3 layers and stack. Add fourth layer. Mix reserved sour cream mixture with whipped topping. Spread on top and sides of cake. Cover and refrigerate for 3 days before serving. *Must be prepared ahead.*

Serves 12

Toffee Ice Cream Cake

An alternate to cheesecake

½ cup butter, melted

10 ounces shortbread cookies, crushed

8 ounces vanilla instant pudding mix

1½ cups milk

2 pints vanilla ice cream, softened

12 ounces frozen whipped topping, thawed

5 ounces chocolate toffee candy bars, crushed

Blend butter and cookie crumbs. Spread on bottom of 13x9 inch dish. Blend pudding mix, milk and ice cream. Spread over crumbs, layer with whipped topping and sprinkle with crushed candy bars. Freeze. Thaw 20 to 25 minutes before serving. *Must be prepared ahead.*

Serves 12

Ritzy Cupcakes

We think they're tops. . .black bottom and all

8 ounces cream cheese, softened

1 egg

⅓ cup sugar

⅛ teaspoon salt

6 ounces semi sweet chocolate chips

1 cup sugar

¼ cup cocoa

1 teaspoon baking soda

½ teaspoon salt

1½ cups flour

1 cup water

⅓ cup salad oil

1 tablespoon vinegar

1 teaspoon vanilla extract

Sliced almonds

With mixer, blend cream cheese, egg, ⅓ cup sugar and salt. Stir in chocolate chips and set aside. In separate bowl, sift remaining 1 cup sugar, cocoa, baking soda, salt and flour. Add water, oil, vinegar and vanilla. Beat until well mixed. Fill paper lined muffin tin cups ⅓ full with chocolate batter. Top each with rounded teaspoon of cream cheese mixture. Sprinkle with almonds. Bake at 350° for 30 minutes or until done. *May be prepared ahead. May be frozen.*

2 dozen

After School Cupcakes

Ideal cooking experience for kids

½ cup butter, softened

1 cup sugar

½ cup peanut butter

2 eggs, beaten

1 cup applesauce

2 cups flour

1 teaspoon baking powder

½ teaspoon salt

½ teaspoon baking soda

6 ounces semi sweet chocolate chips

With mixer, cream butter and sugar. Blend in peanut butter and eggs. Mix in applesauce. Blend in flour, baking powder, salt and baking soda. Gently stir in chocolate chips by hand. Spoon into paper lined muffin tin cups, filling ⅔ full. Bake at 350° for 20 minutes or until brown. Cool on cake racks. *May be prepared ahead. May be frozen.*

2 dozen

Extra Rich Chocolate Chip Cookies

Add milk and a room full of kids

¾ cup sugar

1½ cups brown sugar

1½ cups shortening

3 eggs

½ tablespoon vanilla extract

½ tablespoon salt

½ tablespoon baking soda

3 cups plus 3 tablespoons flour

24 ounces semi sweet chocolate chips

2 cups chopped pecans

With mixer, cream sugars, shortening, eggs and vanilla. Sift salt, baking soda and flour. Blend into creamed mixture. Gently mix in chocolate chips and pecans. Drop by teaspoon onto lightly greased baking sheet and bake at 375° for 8 minutes or until done. *May be prepared ahead. May be frozen.*

6 dozen

Molasses Cookies

Old time Southern recipe renewed

½ cup butter, softened

¾ cup sugar

1 egg

¼ cup molasses

1½ cups flour

¾ teaspoon baking soda

½ teaspoon salt

½ cup raisins

½ cup chopped nuts

½ cup canned shredded coconut

With mixer, cream butter and sugar. Add egg and molasses, beating well. Sift flour with baking soda and salt. Add to creamed mixture and mix well. Stir in raisins, nuts and coconut. Drop by teaspoon onto greased baking sheet and bake at 375° for 8 minutes or until done. *May be prepared ahead. May be frozen.*

3 dozen

Big Boy Cookies
A slice and bake cookie

1 cup shortening
1 cup butter, softened
2 cups brown sugar
2 cups sugar
4 eggs
2 teaspoons vanilla extract
3 cups flour
2 teaspoons salt
2 teaspoons baking soda
3 cups old fashioned oats
2 cups canned shredded coconut
2 cups raisins
1 cup semi sweet chocolate chips
1 cup chopped nuts

With mixer, cream shortening, butter and sugars. Add eggs and vanilla, beating well. Sift flour with salt and baking soda and blend into creamed mixture. Add oats, coconut, raisins, chocolate chips and nuts, stirring well. Shape into roll, wrap in waxed paper and refrigerate overnight. Slice and bake on baking sheet at 350° for 8 minutes or until brown. *Must be prepared ahead. May be frozen.*

7 dozen

Grandma's Sugar Cookies
Thin, crispy and delicious

2 cups sugar
2 cups butter, softened
1 teaspoon salt
1 teaspoon nutmeg
1 teaspoon vanilla extract
2/3 cup buttermilk
1 teaspoon baking soda
5 cups flour
Sprinkles (optional)

With mixer, cream sugar and butter. Blend in salt, nutmeg, vanilla, buttermilk and baking soda. Add flour, 1 cup at a time, mixing well. Chill. Roll and cut into desired shapes. May be decorated with sprinkles. Bake at 375° for 8 minutes or until done. *May be prepared ahead. May be frozen.*

5 dozen

Merry Meringue Christmas Cookies

As pretty as they sound

2 egg whites, room temperature
⅛ teaspoon salt
⅛ teaspoon cream of tartar
¾ cup sugar
½ teaspoon vanilla extract
1 cup semi sweet chocolate chips
1 cup chopped nuts
3 tablespoons crushed peppermint candy

With mixer, beat egg whites in medium bowl until foamy. Add salt and cream of tartar and continue beating until soft peaks form. Add sugar, 1 tablespoon at a time, beating well after each addition. Continue beating until meringue is stiff. Fold in vanilla, chocolate chips, nuts and candy. Drop by teaspoon, ½ inch apart, onto lightly greased baking sheets. Bake at 250° for 40 minutes. Remove to cake racks to cool. *May be prepared ahead. May be frozen.*

5 dozen

Oatmeal Chocolate Chip Cookies

Lunchbox treat

1½ cups brown sugar
½ cup sugar
1 cup plus 2 teaspoons butter, softened
2 eggs
2 teaspoons vanilla extract
1½ cups flour
1 teaspoon baking soda
1 teaspoon salt
1 teaspoon baking powder
½ cup Grapenuts cereal
2¼ cups old fashioned oats
1 cup chopped pecans
12 ounces semi sweet chocolate chips

With mixer, cream sugars with butter. Beat in eggs then vanilla. Sift flour with baking soda, salt and baking powder and add to creamed mixture, mixing well. Stir in cereal, oats, pecans and chocolate chips. Drop by teaspoon onto baking sheets. Bake at 350° for 5 minutes or until brown. *May be prepared ahead. May be frozen.*

7 dozen

Cut Out Cookies
Holiday fun

1 cup butter, softened
1 cup sugar
2 eggs
1 tablespoon milk
1 teaspoon vanilla extract
3 cups flour, sifted
1 tablespoon baking powder
Frosting (optional)

With mixer, cream butter and sugar. Add eggs, milk and vanilla and beat well. Blend in flour and baking powder. Chill dough for 10 minutes. Roll and cut into desired shapes. Bake on baking sheet at 375° for 10 minutes. May be spread with favorite frosting. *May be prepared ahead. May be frozen.*

2 dozen

Scotch Cookies
Old world favorite

½ cup butter, softened
½ cup sugar
1 egg yolk
1¼ cups flour
¼ teaspoon salt
¼ teaspoon vanilla extract
¼ cup sugar
1 teaspoon cinnamon

With mixer, cream butter and ½ cup sugar. Beat in egg yolk, flour, salt and vanilla. Mix remaining ¼ cup sugar with cinnamon in small bowl. Measure dough by teaspoon and shape into balls. Roll in cinnamon and sugar mixture. Place on baking sheet and press with thumb. Bake at 375° for 10 minutes or until brown. *May be prepared ahead. May be frozen.*

3 dozen

Pecan Chewies
Can't stop

4 eggs
1½ cups flour
1 teaspoon baking powder
1 pound brown sugar
1 cup chopped pecans

With mixer, beat eggs until foamy. Blend in flour, baking powder and sugar. Fold in pecans. Bake in 2 greased 13x9 inch baking dishes at 350° for 15 minutes or until brown. Cool and cut into bars. *May be prepared ahead. May be frozen.*

Serves 24

Surprise No Bake Cookies

Nourishing snack you'll repeat

1 cup graham crackers crumbs

2 cups old fashioned oats

2 cups sugar

2 tablespoons cocoa

½ cup milk

½ cup butter

½ cup peanut butter

1 teaspoon vanilla extract

Mix cracker crumbs with oats. Set aside. In large saucepan over medium heat, stir sugar, cocoa, milk and butter until dissolved. Bring mixture to a boil and cook for 1 minute. Remove from heat and stir in peanut butter and vanilla until dissolved. Quickly blend in cracker mixture. Drop by teaspoon onto waxed paper. Cool. *May be prepared ahead.*

6 dozen

Slice and Bake Oatmeal Cookies

A perennial favorite that freezes

1 cup butter, softened

1 cup brown sugar

1 cup sugar

1 teaspoon vanilla extract

2 eggs

1½ cups flour

1 teaspoon salt

1 teaspoon baking soda

3 cups old fashioned oats

With mixer, cream butter and sugars. Add vanilla and eggs, beating well. Mix in flour, salt and baking soda. Stir in oats. Cover and chill. Divide dough and shape into 4 rolls. Wrap individually in waxed paper and freeze. To bake, slice dough into desired thickness and bake at 350° for 10 minutes or until done. *Must be prepared ahead.*

5 to 6 dozen

Rebel Bars

One after another

1 cup butter, softened
2 cups brown sugar
2 eggs
2½ cups flour
3 cups quick oats
1 teaspoon salt
1 teaspoon baking powder
2 teaspoons vanilla extract
12 ounces semi sweet chocolate chips
1 cup sweetened condensed milk
2 teaspoons butter
2 teaspoons vanilla extract
1 cup chopped pecans

With mixer, cream 1 cup butter and brown sugar. Blend in eggs, flour, oats, salt, baking powder and 2 teaspoons vanilla. Spread ⅔ of mixture in 13x9 inch baking dish. In saucepan, melt chocolate chips in condensed milk. Mix in 2 teaspoons butter, 2 teaspoons vanilla and pecans. Spread over flour mixture in baking dish and sprinkle with remaining flour mixture. Bake at 325° for 25 minutes or until done. *May be prepared ahead. May be frozen.*

3 dozen

Friendship Bars

Elementary, yet outstanding

1 pound brown sugar
2 cups Bisquick
4 eggs, well beaten
2 cups chopped pecans

Combine all ingredients, mixing well. Pour into greased 13x9 inch baking dish. Bake at 325° for 30 minutes or until done. Cool and cut into bars. *Must be prepared ahead.*

Serves 12

Graham Cracker Sandwich Bars

Layered dessert you must try

1 pound graham crackers, divided

2 cups butter

2 cups sugar

2 eggs, beaten

⅛ teaspoon salt

1 cup sweetened condensed milk

2 cups graham cracker crumbs

2 cups canned shredded coconut

2 cups chopped pecans

2 teaspoons vanilla extract

Frosting

½ cup butter, melted

3 cups confectioners' sugar, sifted

⅛ teaspoon salt

1 teaspoon vanilla extract

Evaporated milk

Arrange graham crackers in same direction to line 2 (15x10 inch) jelly roll pans. In saucepan, bring butter, sugar, eggs, salt and milk to a boil over medium heat. Stir and cook until thickened. Remove from heat and add cracker crumbs, coconut, pecans and vanilla, stirring well. Pour mixture over graham crackers and top with second layer of graham crackers. Press into place. Spread on frosting, cover and refrigerate for at least 12 hours. *Must be prepared ahead.*

Serves 24

Blend butter, sugar, salt and vanilla. Add enough evaporated milk to make spreadable.

Chocolate Cherry Bars

Tops in eating pleasure

18 ounces chocolate fudge cake mix
21 ounces cherry pie filling
1 teaspoon almond extract
2 eggs, beaten

In large bowl, combine cake mix, pie filling, almond extract and eggs, stirring gently to mix. Pour into greased and floured 13x9 inch baking dish and bake according to cake mix directions. Cool and frost. *Must be prepared ahead.*

Serves 12

Frosting

1 cup sugar
5 tablespoons butter
⅓ cup milk
6 ounces semi sweet chocolate chips

Blend sugar, butter and milk in small saucepan. Bring to a boil, stirring continuously, and cook for 1 minute. Remove from heat and blend in chocolate chips.

Blond Brownies

. . .sans chocolate

4 tablespoons butter
1 cup brown sugar
1 egg
1 teaspoon vanilla extract
½ cup flour
1 teaspoon baking powder
½ teaspoon salt
½ cup chopped nuts

In saucepan, melt butter and add sugar. Stir until dissolved and set aside to cool. Beat egg and vanilla. Mix with butter mixture. Sift flour, baking powder and salt. Blend with butter and egg mixture. Stir in nuts. Pour into greased 11x7 inch baking dish and bake at 350° for 25 minutes. Cool before cutting. *May be prepared ahead.*

Serves 12

French Pie Crust

For the aspiring gourmet. . .a no fail delicate pastry

3 cups flour
1 teaspoon salt
1¼ cups shortening
1 tablespoon vinegar
1 egg
6 tablespoons water

Mix flour and salt. Cut in shortening. Mix until coarsely crumbled. Beat vinegar, egg and water. Blend with crumbs until smooth dough is formed. Divide in ½ and roll out for 2 (9 inch) pie crusts. Prick and bake at 475° for 10 to 15 minutes or fill and bake according to recipe directions. *May be prepared ahead. May be frozen.*

2 (9 inch) crusts

Easy Pie Crust

Trying is believing

½ cup shortening
¼ cup water
¼ teaspoon salt
1 cup flour

In saucepan, bring shortening, water and salt to a boil. With fork, stir in flour until blended. Cool to handling and press into 9 inch pie plate. Prick and bake at 475° for 10 minutes or until done or fill and bake according to recipe directions. For 2 crust pie, double recipe and roll top crust between waxed paper. *May be prepared ahead. May be frozen.*

1 (9 inch) crust

Chocolate Cookie Pie Crust

For ice cream pies

2 cups crumbled chocolate wafer cookies
1½ cups canned shredded coconut
2 tablespoons butter, melted
⅛ teaspoon cinnamon

Blend cookie crumbs, coconut, butter and cinnamon. Press into 9 inch pie plate and bake at 275° for 10 minutes or until done. Cool before filling. *Must be prepared ahead. May be frozen.*

1 (9 inch) crust

Peach Pie

Easier than it should be

6 fresh peaches
1 (9 inch) pie crust
3 egg yolks
⅔ cup sugar
1 tablespoon flour
⅓ cup butter, melted

Slice peaches into pie crust. Blend egg yolks, sugar, flour and butter. Pour over peaches. Bake at 350° for 45 minutes. *May be prepared ahead.*

Serves 8

Sour Cream Apple Pie

Definitely memorable

1 cup sour cream
2 tablespoons flour
¾ cup sugar
¼ teaspoon salt
1 teaspoon vanilla extract
1 egg
3 tart apples, coarsely chopped
1 (9 inch) pie crust

Blend sour cream, flour, sugar and salt. Stir in vanilla, egg and apples. Pour into pie crust and bake at 400° for 25 minutes. Sprinkle with topping and bake for 20 minutes. *May be prepared ahead.*

Serves 8

Topping

⅓ cup flour
½ cup brown sugar
4 tablespoons cold butter

Mix flour and sugar. Cut in butter.

Cherry Pizza

So easy and serves many

½ cup plus 2 tablespoons butter, softened
1 cup flour
2 tablespoons sugar
8 ounces cream cheese, softened
1 cup confectioners' sugar
1 envelope whipped topping mix, prepared
1 teaspoon vanilla extract
21 ounces cherry pie filling

With mixer, cream butter, flour and sugar. Press into pizza pan. Bake at 350° for 10 minutes or until brown. Cool. Blend cream cheese and confectioners' sugar until fluffy. Fold in whipped topping and vanilla. Pour onto crust and top with pie filling. Chill. *Must be prepared ahead.*

Serves 12

Fruit Pizza

Beautiful dessert

¾ cup butter, softened
⅔ cup sugar
½ teaspoon salt
2½ cups flour
⅓ cup milk
8 ounces cream cheese, softened
20 ounces canned crushed pineapple, drained
1½ cups fresh strawberry halves
½ cup slivered almonds
¾ cup canned shredded coconut
1 cup strawberry jelly, melted
Whipped cream

With mixer, cream butter with sugar and salt. Mix in flour and milk and press into pizza pan. Flute and prick crust. Bake for 15 minutes or until golden brown. Cool and spread with cream cheese. Layer with fruits, almonds and coconut. Top with melted jelly and garnish with whipped cream. *Crust may be prepared ahead.*

Serves 12

Mystery Pecan Pie

Sweet tooth satisfaction

8 ounces cream cheese, softened

1 egg

⅓ cup sugar

½ teaspoon vanilla extract

1 (9 inch) pie crust

1 cup pecan halves

2 eggs

¼ cup sugar

⅔ cup dark corn syrup

¼ teaspoon maple flavoring

¼ teaspoon vanilla extract

In medium bowl, combine cream cheese, 1 egg, ⅓ cup sugar and vanilla. Beat with mixer until light and fluffy. Spread on crust and top with pecans. Combine remaining 2 eggs, ¼ cup sugar, corn syrup, maple flavoring and vanilla, mixing well. Gently pour over pecans and bake at 375° for 40 minutes or until done. Chill. *Must be prepared ahead.*

Serves 8

Crustless Coconut Pie

Makes its own surprise crust

4 eggs, beaten

1¾ cups sugar

½ cup self-rising flour

4 tablespoons butter, melted

2 cups milk

1 teaspoon vanilla extract

1⅓ cups canned coconut

Blend eggs, sugar and flour. Mix in butter then milk, vanilla and coconut. Pour into greased 10 inch pie plate and bake at 350° for 30 minutes or until brown. Cool before cutting. *Must be prepared ahead.*

Serves 8

213

Eggnog Pie
A pie from the olden days

3 eggs, separated
½ cup sugar
1 cup milk
1 envelope unflavored gelatin
¼ cup water
¼ cup light rum
¼ cup sugar
1 cup whipping cream, whipped
1 (9 inch) pie crust, baked and cooled
Nutmeg

In double boiler, combine lightly beaten egg yolks, ½ cup sugar and milk. Cook and stir continuously until mixture is thickened. Remove from heat. Dissolve gelatin in water. Stir gelatin and rum into custard, pour into bowl and chill. With mixer, beat egg whites with ¼ cup sugar until soft peaks form. Fold egg whites then whipped cream into custard. Turn into crust and chill. Sprinkle with nutmeg. *Must be prepared ahead.*

Serves 8

Banana Cream Pie
Extra creamy delight

6 tablespoons cake flour
⅔ cup sugar
½ teaspoon salt
1¾ cups milk
2 egg yolks, lightly beaten
¾ teaspoon vanilla extract
1 cup whipping cream, whipped
3 bananas, sliced
1 (9 inch) pie crust, baked

In double boiler, mix flour, sugar, salt, milk, and egg yolks. Heat over boiling water, stirring continuously, until thickened. Remove from heat and cool. Fold in vanilla and whipped cream. In crust, layer ½ of bananas and custard and repeat. Cool. *May be prepared ahead.*

Serves 8

Heavenly Pumpkin Pie

Stir, chill and serve

1 envelope whipped topping mix, prepared

4 ounces vanilla instant pudding mix

½ cup milk

1 teaspoon vanilla extract

16 ounces pumpkin pie filling

2 (9 inch) pie crusts, baked

1 cup whipping cream

2 tablespoons sugar

Nutmeg

Blend topping with pudding mix. Stir in milk, vanilla and pie filling. Pour into pie crusts and chill until set. With mixer, whip cream with sugar, spread over pies and sprinkle with nutmeg. Refrigerate until ready to serve. *Must be prepared ahead. May be frozen.*

Serves 16

Tea House Buttermilk Pie

Pie safe treasure

1 (9 inch) pie crust

3 eggs

1¾ cups sugar

3 tablespoons flour

½ cup butter, softened

1 cup buttermilk

½ tablespoon vanilla extract

Nutmeg to taste

Bake crust at 400° for 10 minutes. Cool. With mixer, blend eggs, sugar, flour and butter. Mix in buttermilk, vanilla and nutmeg. Pour into crust and bake at 350° for 50 minutes or until firm. Cool. *Must be prepared ahead. May be frozen.*

Serves 8

Coffee Ice Cream Pie

Sophisticated dessert

1 ½ cups chocolate cookie crumbs

2 tablepoons sugar

¼ teaspoon cinnamon

5 to 6 tablespoons butter, melted

½ cup sliced almonds

1 quart coffee ice cream, softened

Topping

2 egg whites

⅔ cup sugar

⅓ cup water

½ to 1 cup whipping cream

2 to 3 teaspoons cocoa

Blend cookie crumbs, 2 tablespoons sugar, cinnamon and butter. Stir in almonds. Press into 9 inch pie plate and freeze. Fill crust with ice cream, cover with topping and return to freezer. *Must be prepared ahead.*

Serves 8

Beat egg whites with mixer until stiff. Set aside. Combine ⅔ cup sugar and water in saucepan and heat to thread stage. Pour over egg whites and beat until thickened. Cool. Beat whipping cream with cocoa and fold into egg mixture.

Pralines 'n Cream Pie

A luxury worth indulging

¼ cup brown sugar

1 cup flour

½ cup butter, melted

½ cup chopped pecans

½ gallon vanilla ice cream, softened

12 ounces caramel topping

Blend brown sugar, flour and butter. Mix in pecans. Spread onto greased baking sheet and bake at 325° for 15 minutes. Crumble while hot, then allow to cool. Use ½ to form crust in 2 greased 9 inch pie plates. Top with ice cream and remaining cookie crust mixture. Drizzle with caramel topping, cover and freeze. *Must be prepared ahead.*

Serves 16

Peanut Butter Pie

Goes a long way

8 ounces cream cheese, softened
1½ cups crunchy peanut butter
1 cup milk
1 pound confectioners' sugar
12 ounces frozen whipped topping, thawed
3 graham cracker pie crusts
¼ cup chopped peanuts

With mixer, blend cream cheese, peanut butter, milk and confectioners' sugar until fluffy. Slowly fold in whipped topping. Pour into crusts, sprinkle with peanuts and freeze for at least 8 hours. Serve frozen. *Must be prepared ahead.*

Serves 24

Strawberry Black Bottom Pie

A pie you will be asked to repeat

⅔ cup half and half
6 ounces semi sweet chocolate chips
3 eggs, separated
1 (9 inch) pie crust, baked
1 pint fresh strawberries
2 teaspoons lemon juice
1 envelope unflavored gelatin
¼ cup water
¼ cup sugar
Additional fresh strawberry halves

Heat half and half in saucepan over medium heat. Whisk in chocolate chips until smooth. Remove from heat and add egg yolks, 1 at a time, mixing until well blended. Return to heat. Cook, stirring 1 to 2 minutes longer. Cool and pour into crust. Chill until set. Puree 1 pint strawberries with lemon juice. Soften gelatin in water and stir into puree. Chill until partially congealed. With mixer, beat egg whites, gradually adding sugar, until soft peaks form. Fold in berry mixture then pour over chocolate. Chill until set. To serve, top with additional strawberry halves. *Must be prepared ahead.*

Serves 8

Brownie Bottom Bourbon Pie

Wicked

15 ounces brownie mix, mixed
5 egg yolks
¾ cup sugar
1 envelope unflavored gelatin
¼ cup water
½ cup bourbon, divided
3 cups whipping cream, divided
Salt to taste
½ teaspoon sugar
2 tablespoons chocolate shavings

Bake brownie mix according to package directions in 10 inch pie plate. Cool and set aside. In large bowl with mixer, beat egg yolks well. Slowly beat in ¾ cup sugar. Set aside. In double boiler, soften gelatin in water and stir in ⅓ of bourbon. Heat over boiling water until gelatin is dissolved. Beat into egg mixture. Stir in remaining bourbon. Whip 1 cup whipping cream and fold into mixture. Spread over crust and refrigerate for at least 4 hours. Whip remaining 2 cups whipping cream with salt and ½ teaspoon sugar. Spread over pie and sprinkle with chocolate. *Must be prepared ahead.*

Serves 8

Steamed Christmas Pudding

Will even impress your mother-in-law

½ cup butter, softened
1½ cups brown sugar
2 eggs
1 teaspoon vanilla extract
1 cup flour
1 teaspoon baking soda
¼ teaspoon salt
2 carrots, coarsely chopped
1 apple, coarsely chopped
½ cup raisins
1 cup chopped pecans
1 cup dry bread crumbs
Caramel or hard sauce

With mixer, cream butter and brown sugar. Beat in eggs and vanilla. Sift flour, baking soda and salt and stir into creamed mixture. Fold in carrots, apple, raisins and pecans. Add crumbs and mix well. Spoon into greased heat proof 6 cup mold and cover. Place in steamer or on metal trivet in stockpot. Add water to cover ½ of mold. Bring water to a boil, cover and steam for 3 hours. Serve with sauce. *Must be prepared ahead.*

Serves 12

Swedish Apple Pudding

Flavorful finish for any meal

½ cup butter, softened
2 cups sugar
2 large eggs
½ teaspoon salt
2 cups flour
2 teaspoons baking soda
2 teaspoons cinnamon
5 apples, peeled and finely chopped
Chopped pecans

With mixer, cream butter with sugar, eggs, salt, flour, baking soda and cinnamon. Fold in apples and pour batter into 2 greased and floured 9 inch square cake pans. Sprinkle with pecans. Bake at 350° for 40 minutes. Serve warm with sauce. *Pudding may be prepared ahead.*

Serves 12

Sauce

½ cup butter
½ cup whipping cream
1 cup brown sugar
1 teaspoon vanilla extract

Combine all ingredients in saucepan. Cook and stir until boiling.

Cheese Flan

Complements any Mexican dinner

16 ounces cream cheese, softened
14 ounces sweetened condensed milk
1¾ cups milk
5 eggs
1 cup sugar
2 teaspoons vanilla extract
½ cup sugar

With mixer, blend cream cheese with milks. Beat in 1 egg followed by ¼ cup sugar. Repeat until all eggs and 1 cup sugar are well blended. Mix in vanilla and set aside. Melt remaining ½ cup sugar in small saucepan. Immediately pour into 9 inch springform pan to form caramel base. Top with cream cheese mixture. Place springform pan into larger ovenproof pan filled with 1 inch water. Bake at 350° for 1 hour or until set. Chill in refrigerator before unmolding. *Must be prepared ahead.*

Serves 12

Lime Della Robbia

Light, sweet concoction for hot summer days

1 envelope unflavored gelatin
½ cup sugar
1¼ cups water
1 teaspoon grated lime peel
3 tablespoons lime juice
Green food coloring
3 egg whites
½ cup whipping cream, whipped
Small fresh fruits and berries

In small saucepan, mix gelatin, sugar and water. Heat to boiling, stirring continuously. Mix in lime peel, lime juice and enough food coloring for pale green tint. Refrigerate until partially congealed. With mixer, beat egg whites until soft peaks form. Fold egg whites then whipped cream into gelatin. Pour into greased 4 cup mold. Refrigerate until set. Garnish with wreath of fruits and berries. *Must be prepared ahead.*

Serves 6

Chocolate Kahlua Dessert

Perfect ending for a hearty meal

½ cup butter, melted
1 cup flour
¼ cup brown sugar
½ cup chopped nuts
1 cup confectioners' sugar
8 ounces cream cheese, softened
8 ounces frozen whipped topping, thawed and divided
8 ounces chocolate fudge instant pudding mix
2½ cups milk
½ cup Kahlua
Chocolate shavings

Blend butter, flour and brown sugar. Mix in nuts and press into 13x9 inch baking dish. Bake at 350° for 15 minutes. Cool. With mixer, whip confectioners' sugar, cream cheese and 1 cup whipped topping. Spread over crust and refrigerate for 30 minutes. Mix pudding mix, milk and Kahlua. Spread over cream cheese layer and refrigerate for 30 minutes. Top with remaining whipped topping. Refrigerate overnight. Garnish with chocolate. *Must be prepared ahead.*

Serves 8

Raspberry Mousse

Delicate finale

20 ounces frozen raspberries, slightly thawed
2 cups whipping cream
1 teaspoon grated lime peel
3 tablespoons kirsch
Confectioners' sugar to taste
Lime or kiwi slices

In blender, puree raspberries then strain. Pour strained juice into small saucepan and reduce to 1 cup over low heat. Cool. With mixer, whip cream until soft peaks form. Fold in lime peel, kirsch and sugar. Fold in raspberry juice and chill. Serve in goblets with fruit slices. *Must be prepared ahead.*

Serves 6

Meringue Shells

Create your own gourmet winner

4 egg whites
2/3 cup sugar
1/2 teaspoon vanilla extract
1/3 cup sugar

With mixer, beat egg whites until stiff peaks form. Gradually add 2/3 cup sugar and continue beating until stiff. Fold in vanilla and remaining sugar. Cover baking sheet with heavy brown paper. Spoon meringue onto paper and shape into shells. Bake at 250° for 50 minutes. Serve with your favorite filling. *May be prepared ahead.*

Serves 10

Sherry Custard Pears

Fit for royalty

6 ounces cream cheese, softened
3 tablespoons confectioners' sugar
1/4 cup chopped pecans
2 tablespoons chopped maraschino cherries
1/4 teaspoon almond extract
32 ounces canned pear halves, drained, reserving syrup
Maraschino cherries

With mixer, blend cream cheese with confectioners' sugar. Mix in pecans, cherries and almond extract. Spread over cut sides of 6 pear halves. Top with remaining pears, pressing gently. Place upright in stemmed goblets. Garnish with pieces of cherry to resemble a stem. Pour custard around pears and chill. *Must be prepared ahead.*

Serves 6

Custard

3 ounces non instant vanilla pudding mix
1 1/4 cups milk
1 cup reserved pear syrup
1/4 cup sherry

Mix pudding mix, milk and syrup in saucepan. Cook over medium heat, stirring continuously, until boiling. Remove from heat and stir in sherry. Cool.

Pears in Red Wine

Five star recipe

6 fresh pears
1 teaspoon cornstarch
¼ cup water
2 tablespoons sliced almonds
Whipped cream

Peel pears, leaving stem. Place in syrup in stockpot and simmer, basting frequently, for 20 minutes or until tender. Remove pears and strain syrup. Mix cornstarch with water. Add to syrup and stir until clear. Serve over pears and top with almonds and whipped cream.

Serves 6

Syrup

½ cup plus 2 tablespoons sugar
½ cup water
½ cup Burgundy
1 strip lemon peel
1 cinnamon stick

In stockpot, mix all ingredients. Bring to a boil and cook for 1 minute.

Christmas Apples

An annual treat

¾ cup red hot cinnamon candy
2 cups water
6 apples, peeled and cored
3 ounces cream cheese, softened
2 tablespoons milk
1 teaspoon lemon juice
⅓ cup finely chopped dates
8 ounces canned pineapple chunks, drained
2 tablespoons chopped walnuts

In stockpot, melt candies in water. Add apples and cook over low heat for 10 minutes or until tender, turning frequently. Remove from heat and cool. Turn every hour until apples are deep red. Drain. With mixer, blend cream cheese, milk and lemon juice. Gently stir in dates, pineapple and nuts. Fill apples with cream cheese mixture and chill. *Must be prepared ahead.*

Serves 6

Fresh Peach Melba Torte

Show off summer's bounty

½ cup butter, softened
½ cup sugar
4 eggs, separated
1 cup flour
1 tablespoon baking powder
⅓ cup milk
1 cup sugar
½ cup whipping cream, whipped
2 cups sliced fresh peaches or nectarines, sweetened

With mixer, cream butter and ½ cup sugar. Beat in egg yolks. Sift flour with baking powder. Mix into creamed mixture alternating with milk. Spoon into 2 greased 9 inch springform pans. Beat egg whites until soft peaks form. Add remaining 1 cup sugar, 2 tablespoons at a time, and beat for 30 seconds after each addition. Spread over batter, making swirls. Bake at 325° for 35 to 40 minutes. Cool in pans on cake racks. Remove from pans and put 1 cake layer, meringue side down, on platter. Spread with whipped cream then fruit. Top with remaining layer, meringue side up. Refrigerate for 6 to 8 hours before serving. Serve with Raspberry Sauce. *Must be prepared ahead.*

Serves 8

Raspberry Sauce

½ cup sugar
1 tablespoon cornstarch
2 cups fresh raspberries
1 tablespoon lemon juice

In saucepan, mix sugar and cornstarch. Add ½ of berries, crushing with a spoon. Cook over medium heat until mixture boils and is thickened. Remove from heat and mix in remaining berries and lemon juice. Cool.

English Trifle

An eye catcher

4 ounces vanilla instant pudding mix
2½ cups half and half
12 ladyfingers
¼ cup sherry, divided
1 pint fresh raspberries or strawberries, divided
1 cup whipping cream, whipped

Prepare pudding mix according to package directions, using half and half for milk. Set aside. Line bottom of glass bowl with ladyfingers. Drizzle with sherry, sprinkle with berries and top with part of pudding. Repeat layers, ending with berries, and top with whipped cream. *May be prepared ahead.*

Serves 12

Hot Chocolate Sauce

Beloved of youngsters of all ages

¾ cup sugar
4 tablespoons butter
¼ cup cocoa
2 tablespoons corn syrup
⅛ teaspoon salt
¼ cup milk
2 teaspoons vanilla extract

Combine sugar, butter, cocoa, corn syrup and salt in saucepan and cook over medium heat, stirring until well blended. Mix in milk and bring to a boil, stirring continuously, until thickened. Remove from heat and stir in vanilla. Serve warm. *May be prepared ahead and refrigerated.*

Serves 8

Lemon Sauce

Serve plain or fancy

2 cups sugar
½ cup butter
½ cup lemon juice
3 eggs, well beaten

In saucepan, blend all ingredients. Bring to a boil over medium heat. *May be prepared ahead.*

Serves 8

Raspberry Sauce
Dress up a plain dessert

12 ounces frozen raspberries, thawed

2 1/2 cups miniature marsh-mallows

1 cup whipping cream, whipped

Pour raspberries over marshmallows. Cover and refrigerate overnight. Fold in whipped cream and chill. *Must be prepared ahead.*

Serves 8

Orange and Pineapple Sauce
Delectable ice cream topping

11 ounces canned mandarin oranges, drained, reserving syrup

1 tablespoon cornstarch

8 ounces canned crushed pineapple

1/2 cup orange marmalade

1/2 teaspoon ginger

Blend 1/4 cup reserved orange syrup with cornstarch in saucepan. Stir in pineapple, marmalade and ginger. Cook and stir for 5 minutes or until thickened and bubbly. Stir in oranges. Cool slightly. Serve warm. *May be prepared ahead and refrigerated.*

Serves 10

Creme de Menthe Ice Cream

For that special occasion

12 ounces vanilla wafers, crumbled
4 tablespoons butter, melted
1/2 gallon vanilla ice cream, softened
3/4 cup creme de menthe
10 ounces maraschino cherries, drained, reserving juice

Set aside ¼ cup crumbs and blend remaining crumbs and butter. Press into 13x9 inch dish. Layer ice cream, creme de menthe, ice cream and cherry juice. Repeat until all ingredients are used. Top with remaining crumbs and cherries. Freeze. *Must be prepared ahead and frozen.*

Serves 12

Country Vanilla Ice Cream

Add topping for an old fashioned sundae

2 1/2 cups sugar
6 eggs, beaten
2 cups half and half
4 cups whipping cream
1 quart milk
4 1/2 teaspoons vanilla extract
1/2 teaspoon salt
Additional milk

Gradually add sugar to eggs and beat until stiff. Slowly beat in half and half, whipping cream, milk, vanilla and salt. Pour into ice cream freezer container. Add additional milk to fill if necessary. Freeze. *Must be prepared ahead.*

Serves 8

Tropical Fruit Sherbet

Great ending for an oriental dish

---

3 cups water

3 cups sugar

3 bananas, sliced

16 ounces canned sliced peaches

15 ounces canned pineapple chunks

1¼ cups orange juice

6 tablespoons lemon juice

Heat water, mix in sugar and boil for 5 minutes. Set aside to cool. Mix bananas, peaches, pineapple, orange and lemon juices with sugar mixture. Freeze in ice cream freezer. *Must be prepared ahead.*

Serves 8

Creamy Fruit Freeze

Makes glamorous, easy parfaits

---

12 ounces frozen whipped topping, thawed

14 ounces sweetened condensed milk

20 ounces canned crushed pineapple

21 ounces strawberry pie filling

1 cup chopped nuts

Mix all ingredients and spread in 13x9 inch dish. Freeze. Thaw for 20 minutes before serving. *Must be prepared ahead.*

Serves 12

Lemon Orange Crepes
A scrumptious dessert

3 eggs

1⅓ cups flour

1 tablespoon sugar

⅛ teaspoon salt

1½ cups milk

2 tablespoons butter, melted

1 tablespoon cognac

Oil for frying

Mix eggs, flour, sugar and salt. Add milk, butter and cognac and blend. Heat ½ teaspoon oil in 5 inch crepe pan over medium high heat. Stirring batter each time, pour 2½ tablespoons or just enough batter to cover bottom of pan. Lightly brown on both sides. Remove to clean cloth and cool. Spread filling onto crepes and roll. Place seam side down in greased 13x9 inch baking dish. Cover with sauce and heat until bubbly. *Crepes may be prepared ahead and stacked, covered and refrigerated. May freeze if stacked with waxed paper between each crepe.*

Serves 8

Filling

4 tablespoons butter, softened

8 ounces cream cheese, softened

2 tablespoons sugar

1 teaspoon vanilla extract

1 teaspoon grated lemon peel

With mixer, cream butter and cream cheese. Add sugar, vanilla and lemon peel, blending until light and fluffy.

Sauce

⅔ cup orange marmalade

⅓ cup orange juice

2 tablespoons butter

1 tablespoon lemon juice

½ tablespoon grated lemon peel

Mix all ingredients in saucepan over medium heat. Heat to a gentle boil and cook for 5 minutes or until thickened.

Caramel Popcorn

Makes popcorn special

1 cup brown sugar
¼ cup corn syrup
½ teaspoon salt
½ cup butter
½ teaspoon baking soda
15 cups popped popcorn
Nuts (optional)

Mix brown sugar, corn syrup, salt and butter in saucepan. Cook until bubbly then simmer for 5 minutes. Remove from heat. Add baking soda and stir until mixture foams. Pour over popcorn and mix well. Spread on 2 large greased baking sheets and bake at 200°, stirring every 15 minutes, for 1 hour. For variation, add nuts. *May be prepared ahead.*

Serves 20

Pecan Pralines

Marshmallows are the difference

1½ cups sugar
½ cup brown sugar
5 ounces evaporated milk
2 tablespoons corn syrup
Salt to taste
4 tablespoons butter
6 large marshmallows
2 cups chopped pecans

In large saucepan, boil sugar, brown sugar, evaporated milk and corn syrup until mixture reaches soft ball stage. Mix in salt, butter and marshmallows, stirring until dissolved. Add pecans and stir until mixture begins to stiffen. Drop by tablespoon onto waxed paper. *May be prepared ahead.*

Serves 20

Creamy Pralines

Improve with age if they last

½ cup butter

1 pound brown sugar

2 cups sugar

1 cup sour cream

1 cup whipping cream

Salt to taste

2 teaspoons vanilla extract

2¼ cups chopped pecans

In saucepan, melt butter over low heat. Stir in sugars until dissolved. Blend in sour cream, whipping cream and salt. Cook, stirring continuously, until well blended. Increase heat to medium and cook, stirring continuously, to soft ball stage. Remove from heat and cool for 10 minutes. Add vanilla and pecans. Beat until well blended. Drop by teaspoon onto waxed paper and cool. *May be prepared ahead. May be frozen.*

Serves 20

Salt Water Taffy Pull

Teenagers' specialty

2 tablespoons butter

4 cups sugar

⅔ cup boiling water

⅓ cup vinegar

Salt to taste

Melt butter in large saucepan. Add sugar, water, vinegar and salt. Stir until sugar dissolves. Boil for 30 minutes or until soft crack stage. Turn onto greased surface and cool to handling. With lightly greased hands, pull taffy until white. Cut into cubes. *May be prepared ahead.*

Serves 20

Butternut Candy

A holiday recipe to share

2 cups unsalted butter
2 cups sugar
1 cup sliced almonds
1 cup chopped pecans

In saucepan, melt butter over medium high heat. Add sugar and bring to a boil, stirring continuously. Boil and stir to hard crack stage. Slowly mix in nuts and continue boiling. Turn onto greased baking sheet and score. Cool and crack along scored lines. *Must be prepared ahead.*

Serves 20

Kentucky Colonels

When friends drop by

¾ cup chopped pecans
7 tablespoons bourbon
½ cup butter, softened
1 pound confectioners' sugar
¼ block paraffin
7½ ounces German's sweet chocolate

Soak pecans in bourbon overnight. With mixer, cream butter and sugar. Slowly mix in pecan mixture and stir well. Shape into small balls and place on waxed paper lined baking sheets. Cover with waxed paper and freeze. Melt paraffin and chocolate in double boiler. Dip balls in chocolate and harden on waxed paper. *Must be prepared ahead. May be frozen.*

Serves 20

Chocolate Peanut Butter Balls

Betcha can't eat just one

2 cups peanut butter

1 pound confectioners' sugar

3 cups Rice Krispies cereal, crushed

½ cup butter, melted

10 ounces chocolate candy bars

6 ounces semi sweet chocolate chips

⅓ block paraffin

Blend peanut butter, confectioners' sugar and cereal. Pour butter over mixture. Mix well and roll into 1 inch balls. Refrigerate overnight. Melt chocolates with paraffin. Dip balls into chocolate mixture and place on waxed paper to harden. *Must be prepared ahead.*

Serves 20

Yummy Creamy Fudge

Simple and delicious

14 ounces sweetened condensed milk

12 ounces semi sweet chocolate chips

¾ cup chopped pecans

In saucepan, stir milk and chocolate chips over low heat until chocolate is melted. Stir in pecans and pour into greased 8 inch square dish. Cool before cutting.

Serves 10

White Chocolate Cranberries

True to its name

1 pound white chocolate

12 ounces fresh cranberries

Melt chocolate in double boiler over low heat. Dip cranberries in chocolate, place on waxed paper lined dish and refrigerate to harden. *Must be prepared ahead.*

Serves 10

Kahlua Nuts

Plan on seconds

¾ *cup brown sugar*

¼ *cup Kahlua*

2 *tablespoons brandy*

1 *tablespoon corn syrup*

1½ *cups pecan halves*

Confectioners' sugar

Blend brown sugar, Kahlua, brandy and corn syrup. Add pecans and mix until well coated. Roll in confectioners' sugar, and place on waxed paper to harden. *Must be prepared ahead.*

Serves 10

Sherried Walnuts

For holiday gift giving

2½ *cups walnut halves*

1½ *cups sugar*

½ *cup sherry*

½ *teaspoon cinnamon*

Place nuts on baking sheet. Heat at 350°, stirring every 5 minutes, until brown. In saucepan, blend sugar and sherry. Boil until soft ball stage. Remove from heat, add cinnamon and nuts and stir until nontransparent. Turn onto greased surface. Break into small pieces while warm. *May be prepared ahead.*

Serves 10

Index

A

B

238

G

H

Junior League of Richardson, Inc.
P.O. Box 835808
Richardson, Texas 75083

NAME _____

ADDRESS _____

CITY _____ STATE _____ ZIP _____

Please send me _____ copies of
PLAIN AND FANCY @ $15.00 each   _____

Postage and Handling @ $2.00 each   _____

Sales Tax for Texas residents   _____

    TOTAL   _____

Checks payable to the Junior League of Richardson

Please charge to my: ☐ **VISA**   ☐ **MASTERCARD**

CARD NO. ☐☐☐☐☐☐☐☐☐☐☐☐☐☐☐☐

EXPIRATION DATE _____

SIGNATURE OF CARD HOLDER _____

- -

PLAIN & Fancy

Junior League of Richardson, Inc.
P.O. Box 835808
Richardson, Texas 75083

NAME _____

ADDRESS _____

CITY _____ STATE _____ ZIP _____

Please send me _____ copies of
PLAIN AND FANCY @ $15.00 each   _____

Postage and Handling @ $2.00 each   _____

Sales Tax for Texas residents   _____

    TOTAL   _____

Checks payable to the Junior League of Richardson

Please charge to my: ☐ **VISA**   ☐ **MASTERCARD**

CARD NO. ☐☐☐☐☐☐☐☐☐☐☐☐☐☐☐☐

EXPIRATION DATE _____

SIGNATURE OF CARD HOLDER _____

PLAIN & Fancy

Junior League of Richardson, Inc.
P.O. Box 835808
Richardson, Texas 75083

NAME _____

ADDRESS _____

CITY _____ STATE _____ ZIP _____

Please send me _____ copies of
PLAIN AND FANCY @ $15.00 each   _____

Postage and Handling @ $2.00 each   _____

Sales Tax for Texas residents   _____

    TOTAL   _____

Checks payable to the Junior League of Richardson

Please charge to my: ☐ **VISA**   ☐ **MASTERCARD**

CARD NO. ☐☐☐☐☐☐☐☐☐☐☐☐☐☐☐☐☐

EXPIRATION DATE _____

SIGNATURE OF CARD HOLDER _____

- -

PLAIN & Fancy

Junior League of Richardson, Inc.
P.O. Box 835808
Richardson, Texas 75083

NAME _____

ADDRESS _____

CITY _____ STATE _____ ZIP _____

Please send me _____ copies of
PLAIN AND FANCY @ $15.00 each   _____

Postage and Handling @ $2.00 each   _____

Sales Tax for Texas residents   _____

    TOTAL   _____

Checks payable to the Junior League of Richardson

Please charge to my: ☐ **VISA**   ☐ **MASTERCARD**

CARD NO. ☐☐☐☐☐☐☐☐☐☐☐☐☐☐☐☐☐

EXPIRATION DATE _____

SIGNATURE OF CARD HOLDER _____